YOU GOTTA BELIEVE!

YOU GOTTA BELIEVE!

GEORGE SHINN

Tyndale House Publishers, Inc.
WHEATON, ILLINOIS

Library of Congress Cataloging-in-Publication Data

Shinn, George.
  You gotta believe! / George Shinn with Jim Nelson Black.
    p. cm.
  ISBN 0-8423-8584-3 (alk. paper)
    1. Shinn, George. 2. Basketball players—United States—Biography. 3. Basketball players—
United States—Religious life. 4. Christian life—United States. 5. Charlotte Hornets
(Basketball team) I. Black, Jim Nelson. II. Title.
796.323′092—dc20
[B]   95-38527

Printed in the United States of America

01 00 99 98 97 96
7   6   5   4   3   2   1

CONTENTS

PREFACE

George Shinn's Charlotte Hornets are a team of destiny.

That's what people are saying. And for the thousands of fans and dozens of sportswriters who follow this team, the Hornets are taking on the dimensions of legend—something like the Cowboys in football or the Dodgers in baseball. They are becoming America's team.

It's not just the purple-and-teal Alexander Julian uniforms; it's not just the personality of superstar players like Larry Johnson, Glen Rice, and Muggsy Bogues. It's something else: some character, some feeling, some star quality that makes this ball club unique and keeps people tuning in to see how they're playing. A lot of people who don't care a thing about professional basketball are drawn to this franchise because of that whatever-it-is that makes the Hornets of Charlotte so unique.

Their fifty-win season in 1994–95 punctuated their meteoric rise, earning them a second trip to the play-offs in just seven short years. They vaulted past the Chicago Bulls to top the list in NBA merchandise sales during that same season, proving that purple and teal is the deal from Charlotte to Shanghai. The team has entertained sellout crowds at all but 5 of their 287 home games, packing the league's largest arena with some of the sports world's most energetic fans.

The Hornets' tremendous popularity has been a key element in Charlotte's emergence as a major league city. Their six NBA attendance championships and their huge following played a major role in the NFL's recent decision to expand to the Carolinas. The city of Charlotte has developed into one of the nation's fastest-growing financial centers, its expansion virtually paralleling the growth of its favorite attraction—the Hornets.

But where did it all start?

When George Shinn entered the race to acquire an NBA franchise, one reporter trumpeted, "The only franchise that Charlotte, North Carolina, will get will be the one with golden arches." That joke may well have reflected many people's feelings at the time. After all, George was still a relative unknown, a young businessman from North Carolina, and Charlotte was easily the smallest city in the running for an NBA franchise. But the joke was on the reporters and the naysayers who doubted him. Not only did George win the franchise, but Charlotte was the first expansion city chosen by the NBA's franchise committee.

Anyone who knows George Shinn will tell you never to sell him short. He has a record of persistence, dogged determination, and infectious optimism that has brought him an incredible string of successes over the years. When the doubts and insults sting the most, George just works that much harder. Most of the time, his long shots turn out to be the game winners.

The George Shinn story has been told in many ways and in many places, but never quite like this. This is George Shinn's life story in his own words—the story of a small-town boy who took stock of his assets and liabilities at an early age, laid out his objectives, and went on to achieve remarkable success in life.

This is also the story of a man of strong convictions. George's sense of faith is one of the most distinctive aspects of his personality. He has a sincere religious faith as well as an abiding faith in other people, a deep commitment to his home state, and an unwavering sense of purpose in life. From the first, George was determined to hold fast to the things that really matter, to the permanent things, and to share his success with others.

As you come to know him better in these pages, perhaps

you will find that his enthusiasm and determination are contagious. Really believing, George says, means doing something to make the world a better place, and he says we all share in the responsibility of making America a better place to live and raise our families. Opportunity is key, and opportunity belongs to everybody. If anybody believes the truth of that statement, it's George Shinn. And, as he says, you *gotta* believe!

The Editors

1

Stand Back and Watch!

BASKETBALL and North Carolina. Most people would say they go together, but considering the trouble I had trying to convince some folks in my home state that it was a good idea to bring a professional basketball team to Charlotte, you would have thought they had nothing in common. There seemed to be critics in every corner in the early days, shooting at me and telling anyone who would listen how ridiculous it was for George Shinn to go after an NBA franchise.

One of the legendary coaches in our area, a man who had coached at Wake Forest and was considered one of the top experts in the game, said I was out of my mind. He said

1

professional basketball would never work in Charlotte. We'd bomb out, he said, and besides that, it was just plain dumb. He was so incredibly negative I had to wonder how a guy who loved the game as much as he did could say such things. But that was the kind of environment I had to face almost every day when we first started out.

Fortunately, overcoming long odds is nothing new for me. I've been doing it all my life. And for a guy who finished dead last in a high school class of 232 people, I had plenty of reasons to develop a little motivation. For the longest time I thought school was just a place to have fun, to meet friends, to play sports, or to hang out until you were ready to get a job. But eventually the truth caught up with me.

One of the legendary coaches in our area, a man who had coached at Wake Forest and was considered one of the top experts in the game, said I was out of my mind.

Later, when I discovered that commitment, determination, hard work, and self-discipline could change the quality of my life and help me accomplish the things I really wanted in life, I made up my mind that I was going to be the best I could be. But that's just part of the story.

On the way to building a string of successful businesses, I learned a lot of things about myself. I came to understand what it would take to get ahead. Growing up in a small town, losing my father at the age of eight, and learning to live with only the barest necessities for many years taught me even more. I learned that faith in God is essential and that perseverance, loyalty, and honesty are the building blocks of success in any field.

Those were among the most important values my mother ever taught me as a child. They are still just as important to me today as they were then. I learned that life is about people, and the best kind of life is one in which you are involved with the people around you in ways that will bring happiness and success to everyone.

Whenever people ask me to speak at public events, they usually want to hear about the Charlotte Hornets and our success as a team. It is a pretty remarkable story. The way we built the team from scratch, went through the early growing pains, and suddenly earned our way into the NBA play-offs in only our fifth year in the league is pretty dramatic. The media have followed us every step of the way, and a lot of the best stories have been told in print. But the real story—the one behind the ones you see in the newspapers—is the story of how a positive attitude, hard work, sincere faith, and the help of a lot of good people laid the foundations for everything we've accomplished in Charlotte. That's the story I want to tell in this book.

The Road to the NBA
When I think about all the changes that have taken place in the past ten years, I sometimes find it hard to believe, myself. It's a long, hard road from Kannapolis, North Carolina, to the NBA. What we have accomplished here didn't happen overnight, and it didn't happen by accident. It was a deliberate plan. While I was always examining my options and considering just which way I should turn in each situation, I always had a pretty good idea where I'd end up. I knew that, one way or the other, I wanted to be part of bringing a top-notch national sports franchise to my home state.

My first love when I was growing up was baseball, so when I first started thinking about acquiring a team, I looked into Major League Baseball. A friend of mine set up a meeting for me in the spring of 1985 with Bowie Kuhn in New York, and I flew up and had lunch with him. I wanted to get a feel for what it would take to bring an expansion team to our area. Kuhn, who was the former baseball commissioner, knew what was going on around the league. He also knew the decision-making structure in intimate detail.

While I was in New York, I also went to see Peter Uberroth,

3

who was commissioner at that time. I wanted to see what he thought my chances might be of getting a team. He told me he thought it was probably a waste of time. He wasn't so bold as to say it was a *complete* waste of time. But he told me that Charlotte might be able to get a major league team in twenty years, if I was really serious.

If we really wanted to get a team in twenty years, he told me, we should go ahead and invest now in another team as a minority partner. "Learn the ropes," Uberroth said. "Get to be an insider, and you'll be in a much better position to get a team when your city's large enough." Uberroth and Kuhn both felt Charlotte was not large enough at that time to support a Major League Baseball franchise.

I didn't believe them at first. I thought it was just a gentle put-off. But now I believe they were absolutely right. To get the kinds of crowds we would need in order to keep a big-league team afloat, we would need a much larger centralized market than we currently have.

> I didn't give up. I just started looking in other directions.

When a major league team is on a home stand, they may play for ten days straight and sometimes with doubleheaders and other special events that demand capacity crowds. You can't expect fans who live a hundred miles away to drive to Charlotte more than once or twice a week. A working person who drives in for a game on Wednesday night, for example, can't get home in time to get some rest, get up the next morning, and be ready for work the next day.

After I thought about it for a while, I realized that Peter was telling me the truth. And I realized that, for the moment at least, pursuing a baseball franchise would be a waste of time. But I didn't give up. I just started looking in other directions.

I read somewhere that one of the main reasons Napoleon Bonaparte was such a brilliant military strategist was that he always had a backup plan in case things went wrong with his first approach. If his troops couldn't take the city or if they began taking too many casualties, he would turn to plan B, which he had already mapped out the night before. Well, I took that lesson to heart, and when I could see that my hopes for a baseball franchise had to be put on hold, I went over to see David Stern, the commissioner of the NBA. That was my backup plan for the trip to New York.

I had already called ahead to Stern's office and arranged to meet with him, and when we got together, I told him I wanted to know what it would take to bring an NBA team to Charlotte. Unlike the gentlemen I had spoken to earlier that day, Stern didn't close the door on me. He recognized the close connection between North Carolina and basketball, and he told me the league was already considering a possible expansion. If I was truly interested, he said, they could give me a packet of information on the NBA along with an expansion application, which I could submit after I put together my business plan and the other details they would need. That was all I needed to hear.

In the Public Eye

To make things even more interesting, the media in Charlotte somehow got wind of my plans and followed me up to New York. They wanted to know everything that was going on and whether or not there was already a deal in the works to bring a team to our city. The newspapers and the broadcast media were full of stories about George Shinn's trip to New York, and everybody was speculating on whether or not I would be successful.

As you can imagine, when I went back to the NBA a few weeks later with a $100,000 check and the application forms all filled out, the reporters were out in droves, and you better believe there was a sense of excitement and expectation in the air. That was really good for the people of Charlotte. It helped them get into the spirit of what was going on.

For added impact, I took Governor Jim Martin and the mayor of Charlotte, Harvey Gantt, along with me to the meeting in New York to indicate to David Stern and the other

5

team owners just how serious we were about getting a franchise. From start to finish, we put together a plan designed to convince the league that Charlotte was absolutely the right place to expand and that we meant business.

The element of the plan that got the most attention from the media—and which also caused the greatest controversy and the longest delays—was the lease I negotiated for use of the new Charlotte Coliseum. I wanted to show the league how committed the citizens of Charlotte were to this idea, so I negotiated an agreement to use the facility for $1 per game.

The taxpayers had already voted to build the new sports center even before there was any thought of getting a team. They were hoping to attract the Atlantic Coast Conference (ACC) tournament, the NCAA regionals, and possibly the Final Four, as well as other events of that sort. But the fact that the largest indoor arena in the country was already in the process of being built and the fact that we had already locked up a good lease agreement had just the right effect. It especially caught the eyes of the other team owners.

What the NBA didn't see, however, were all the battles with the coliseum authority. Some of the people operating it were convinced that professional sports teams would never succeed in Charlotte. Pro sports hadn't succeeded here in the past, they reasoned, so how could anyone expect them to succeed now? On top of that, their experience with sports franchises, coliseum leases, and all the other businesses connected with professional and minor league sports said that they were either "slow pay or no pay." That's the attitude I was up against from the very beginning.

In order to get a feel for sports management, however, and to see how the citizens of North Carolina would react to professional sports, I arranged to bring in two United States Football League (USFL) teams to play an exhibition game in Charlotte. On two occasions I put together all the arrangements, contracted for all the services we would need, leased the facilities, and paid all the various fees and licenses. On top of that, we sold tickets in advance to guarantee the revenues needed to satisfy our contracts with the USFL. Both games were fun and successful, and we even made a little money on the events. But most important, this experience laid the foundation for bringing professional sports to our area.

When we held those exhibition games, I made it a point to pay everybody in thirty days or less. I did that intentionally to deflate the rumors that minor league teams had never paid their bills on time. From the start, I made sure that I established myself as being dependable, trustworthy, and a man who keeps his word.

What I really needed, however, was somebody with a little vision to sit down and talk to me about my plans—somebody who could help me get the lease and put together a plan that would be a win-win situation, both for the city and for me. Fortunately, we had a very perceptive mayor in Harvey Gantt, who is one of the state's outstanding citizens. The first black student at Clemson University, Harvey gained national attention when he ran for the Senate against Jesse Helms. He didn't win that race, but he is a man of great vision and is a talented leader. I have always held Harvey in the highest regard.

> *From the start, I made sure that I established myself as being dependable, trustworthy, and a man who keeps his word.*

At one point in our deliberations, Harvey sat down with me and said, "George, what would it take for you to get that franchise for Charlotte?" I smiled. Finally, I had someone who understood the situation. I said, "Harvey, the owners of all the other NBA teams will eventually vote on who gets this franchise. If I can show them that I've got a lease that's a real sweetheart deal, that's going to be a big help in getting the team." We talked about all the various options. Obviously I wanted the building rent free, but I also thought the team needed to control concessions, parking, and everything else, for that matter.

During our conversation, I discovered that concessions

and parking are almost always considered sacred cows by the people who run the major sports arenas around the country. Harvey said, "George, what if we could put together a deal where you basically got the building rent free, but all the parking and concessions would go to the coliseum authority?"

By this time I could see that was going to be the best option for everyone, so I agreed. And after I thought about the implications of that arrangement, I added, "You know, Harvey, if we do it that way, I'm going to have to work a little harder to sell more tickets. And all the tickets we sell over a certain number will be profit. So our success is really in our own hands. The more people we bring to the coliseum, the more parking the city can sell . . . and the more food the fans will buy!" I thought that would be a good foundation for our future relationship with the city.

Getting the Word Out
Even though the logic was simple enough, it still took some serious discussions and a lot of time to convince the coliseum authority to go along with those terms. Today, I thank God for Harvey Gantt, for his remarkable perception, and for the fact that he trusted me enough to stand behind those plans and proposals. He was one of our biggest cheerleaders when we needed all the help we could get. And I'm also proud to say that Harvey Gantt bought the very first season ticket.

The fact that we were bringing professional basketball to North Carolina should have been a positive for everyone. Even though everybody knows the Tarheel State is big on basketball, for some reason the politicians and sportswriters didn't see it that way. When I tried to use our state's passion for this game as a selling tool, some of those people said, "Sure, George, North Carolinians love their basketball. But it's college basketball! They don't like pro ball."

The Carolina Cougars had played in Charlotte for a while. They were an American Basketball Association (ABA) team, but Charlotte was not really their home. They played in three cities: Raleigh, Greensboro, and Charlotte. The problem was that nobody could decide whose team they were. Where did they belong? Which was their home crowd? Nobody felt a sense of ownership.

I suppose some of the complainers had a right to be skeptical based on that kind of experience, but we were proposing to do something completely new and different. I believed that if people loved Michael Jordan during the three years he played at the University of North Carolina—and they really did love to watch him play—then why not watch him play for the next ten to fifteen years in the NBA?

Not all the great players in basketball come from the Atlantic Coast Conference schools. There are great ones all over this country. And the best of the best end up in the NBA. To say that people only like amateur sports, to say that they wouldn't like professional basketball just as much, didn't make sense to me. If people in North Carolina loved the game of basketball and if they liked

> I believe the real difference was my commitment, enthusiasm, and drive.

seeing the greatest athletes in the world come here to compete, then they were going to love having an NBA team of their own.

Despite my best arguments, I finally had to go before the full city council to get our lease agreement approved. The coliseum authority, which is an independent board, would not go along. I spoke in support of the lease agreement, and Martin Brackett, who was the spokesman for the coliseum authority, argued for more stringent terms. I'm happy to say that even though Brackett was a trained trial lawyer and made a strong argument, our request was eventually approved and we got the lease we needed.

Harvey Gantt had proposed a winning compromise, and I had offered my best arguments. But I believe the real difference was my commitment, enthusiasm, and drive. When it was finally settled, Al Russo, mayor pro tem, came up to me and said, "George, I could see you were really uptight about all this. At one point you said, 'Won't somebody here just trust me?' When I heard those words I made up my mind. I said to myself, 'Yes, George, I'll trust you!'" He said there were others on the city council who felt the same way.

Today, they're all glad they made that decision. If they hadn't, there's a good chance we would not have gotten the franchise. Charlotte still wouldn't have a professional team, and the coliseum would be a massive white elephant, draining off thousands of taxpayer dollars every single day. And Mecklenburg County, which has grown dramatically in the past five years, would not have all the opportunities and benefits it now has.

Today, we have not just a professional sports franchise but unlimited growth potential. The Charlotte Hornets have helped put our city on the map, and it's hard to believe how close we came to missing out on all of that.

2

Against the Odds

WITH all I had to do to get ready for my next trip to New York, it took several weeks to put all the pieces together. But before long my colleagues and I got the details worked out, and I went back to the league office in New York to make the preliminary presentation. We went through the preliminaries step-by-step and passed all the initial qualification requirements. Then came the time for the first full-fledged presentation.

Our first attempt to get the attention of the league was to be at the owners' meeting in Phoenix on October 20, 1986. This was where the representatives from the various cities under consideration would come in to make their pitch. The

Charlotte contingent was just one of a large number of groups with hopes of getting a franchise. At one time there were eleven cities trying for a team, and the NBA was only talking about two new slots.

The Phoenix newspaper published a list of the cities that were trying to get franchises. Number one on their list was Minneapolis. The sportswriters projected that, based on all the factors to be considered by the league officials, the first and most likely city to get an expansion team would be Minneapolis. They ranked each city and each prospective owner in order, and in a sidebar, the writers gave the reasons for their choices.

> One of the writers said, "The only franchise Charlotte, North Carolina, will get will be the one with golden arches."

They said that Minnesota had supported the Twins in baseball, the Vikings in football, and the North Stars in hockey. They had also hosted the Final Four, the All-Star Game, and many other major college and professional sporting events for many years. They even pointed out that the original home of the Los Angeles Lakers had been Minnesota—that's how they got the name Lakers in the first place.

Well, as I read down the list I knew that if I was going to find Charlotte I would have to look down to the very bottom of the page. Sure enough, that's where we were. Out of eleven, we were ranked last, and in the comments one of the writers said, "The only franchise Charlotte, North Carolina, will get will be the one with golden arches."

Imagine how I felt after reading those words. It was just a few hours before my big presentation, and we had spent hundreds of hours and hundreds of thousands of dollars preparing for this moment. It sounds funny now—and the golden arches joke has become part of our legend—but at that moment I felt battered and humiliated. I could not have felt any lower.

I had come so far, and my supporters, my prospective co-owners, and our families had already risked so much just in coming to Phoenix. It would have been terrible to lose this opportunity. We had to face reality, but I believed in what we were doing, and I wasn't about to let those remarks or any others cooked up by a bunch of reporters slow us down. There was simply too much at stake.

Once again I thought the situation over and put it behind me. I made up my mind that I was going to go out there and give it my best shot. So what if we were ranked dead last? I had started from that position before! We would bring out our best weapons, show them the research and the market projections we had prepared, along with a fantastic new video about Charlotte put together specifically for this event by Charlotte sports consultant Max Muhleman, and then we would just wait and trust that the right decisions would be made.

I do a lot of public speaking, and I prefer not to use notes. Especially on this occasion, I wanted to come across as naturally as possible. The team owners and executives had to know that I was a real person. I didn't want to give a speech or to refer to notes as I made the presentation, so I stayed up all night in my hotel room going over it, line by line. Long after my wife, Carolyn, had gone to bed, I was still making notes, talking out loud, and practicing all the things I planned to say. I was walking back and forth, rehearsing every part of the presentation and thinking through the visual aids.

After a couple of hours, Carolyn sat up in bed and said she'd had about enough of it. "George, either turn off the light and come to bed," she said, "or if you insist on staying up all night, then go into the bathroom so I can get some rest." So that's what I did. I went into the bathroom and kept on working through the night. I remember standing there in front of the mirror, practicing my hand gestures, trying to decide the best way to get all my points across.

Two other investors had come to Arizona with me—Felix

Sabates and Rick Hendrick. Felix is a colorful guy. He's a sort of turbocharged Ricky Ricardo, and he refers to himself as "the Cuban refugee." He came here from Cuba and has done well in business.

Rick Hendrick was a partner of mine in the automobile business. At one time I had owned five automobile dealerships in North and South Carolina. I owned some of them outright, and I was in partnership with Rick on others. When I finally decided to get out of the car business, I sold my interests to Rick. Today, he is one of the largest volume car and truck dealers in the country. He is also a major success in professional automobile racing, which is huge in North Carolina and nationally, and has three of the top cars and drivers that race on the NASCAR circuit.

In addition to Rick and Felix, I brought along an accountant from Arthur Andersen, the firm working with me on putting together the financial information we would need. When you hire a big-eight accounting firm, it's immediately apparent that you're trying to be as thorough and realistic as possible. You're not putting up any funny numbers, and you're not making any unrealistic promises.

From the very first, we used estimates that we thought would be average for our market. Instead of building our projections on sellout crowds of twenty-four thousand fans, we based them on half that number, on just twelve thousand paying fans. We felt that was the safest and most realistic approach, and we hoped the league would see it that way too.

Out on a Limb

I wanted the numbers to be conservative just to be sure we weren't exaggerating our potential for success. That turned out to be a good business decision, but when the other investors first saw those low estimates, they seemed less than excited about the deal. All of a sudden they were concerned that this thing might not work out, and I was afraid they were going to back out on me. I really needed them to be part of the deal, and if I expected to get the kind of financial backing we were asking for, then I needed them to be committed to what we were doing.

To keep Felix and Rick on the team, I made them an offer. "I know how you guys feel," I told them. "I can see that you're nervous about this thing, and you're worried that we could all lose a lot of money if it doesn't work out. I'm concerned too," I said, "but I'm not as worried about it as you seem to be. I really believe it will work. So if you guys will stick with me and help me land this franchise, I'll agree to protect your financial interests."

I knew I was about to go out on a limb, but I really had faith in what we were doing, so I offered them a "put and call" option, meaning that I would guarantee their up-front investment while reserving a buyout option on the other end. "If we get the franchise and somehow we don't make a go of it," I told them, "all you have to do is call and tell me to, and I'll pay back your entire investment with interest. We'll draw up an agreement that spells out the options on both sides.

> *I knew I was about to go out on a limb, but I really had faith in what we were doing.*

"I have covered all of our out-of-pocket expenses so far, including travel, marketing materials, and all the other development costs. But, in return for protecting your investment," I said, "if we are successful and if we do get the team, then after a reasonable period of time I will have the option of buying out your interest in the team according to the same terms and conditions. Is that fair?" They thought about it and then agreed that it was a good bargain and a fair agreement. The offer would give them the up-front security they wanted and no long-term risks on the other end. So we drafted the agreement and each of us signed it.

At that time we thought the cost of the franchise was going to be about $25 million. We told the owners and league officials about our net worth, and I tried to make them feel comfortable about our ability to pay the franchise fees and that sort of thing.

We had already launched a season-ticket campaign before we went to Phoenix, so we had some idea of what kind of support we could expect from the fans in Charlotte. Several other cities that were trying to get a team had more impressive numbers than we did, but based on my experience in putting on those exhibition games with USFL teams, I had taken a somewhat different approach from the others.

The other teams told their fans that if they would send in $50, they would put their name on a list. Then if the city actually got the franchise, those fans would receive the best tickets available. If they didn't get the franchise, they said, then everybody's money would be refunded.

Well, some cities went wild. Orlando outsold everybody and had more than twenty thousand reservations in hand at the Phoenix meeting.

I decided I wanted some quality in what we were doing, so we launched our campaign by selling tickets based on where the seats would be located in the coliseum. They weren't just reservations, but actual tickets. The highest priced tickets required a deposit of $200 apiece, and the cheapest were $100. The fans were actually paying a deposit on a season ticket.

I told the fans that if they would send in their money, I would reserve their tickets. If we failed to get the team, they'd get all their money back, without interest. But on the other hand, if we did get the team, then their deposit would be applied toward the purchase of a season ticket. We sold more than 7,500 tickets and collected over a million dollars. On the day of my presentation in Phoenix, I brought all those statements with me, with the names and addresses of our potential season-ticket holders, certified by Arthur Andersen.

When we arrived at the conference center, they asked us to wait outside in a little room, where there were soft drinks and refreshments of various kinds, until our turn came. I was nervous, and to make matters worse, there were television cameras and reporters following me everywhere I went. The media were all there—the newspapers, sports magazines, and local and national television. It seemed like the eyes of the entire world were on me. I was there representing not just my city but all the people back home in the Carolinas.

At one point I had to go to the bathroom, and when I walked into the men's room, the television camera came right in there with me, lights on and tape rolling. I turned around and said, "Do you mind? Can I have some privacy in here?"

The cameraman said, "I'm sorry, but we're supposed to follow your every move."

"Well," I said, "this is one move you're not going to follow."

All or Nothing

When I finally got the chance to make my presentation, my mouth was as dry as cotton. The room was full. You talk about athletes having butterflies in their stomach before a big game. I had them too. Big time! But whenever I find myself in a situation like that, I just stop and breathe a little prayer. "God, I need your help," I said. "Be with me."

The first thing I did was introduce myself and my partners. "Gentlemen," I said, "this is our ownership group. There won't be twenty-five of us; it's just us. And there won't be any out-of-town owners in the group, either. We're all local. We can't go anywhere." At that point there were four investors: Rick Hendrick, Felix Sabates, another businessman—Cy Bahakel, who had joined us—and me. After we went through part of the business plan, I showed them the video Max Muhleman had put together for us. Max had done an outstanding job, and the owners were extremely impressed by what they learned about our city.

Max is one of the most creative people I know, and he deserves a lot of credit for helping us land the Hornets franchise. His company is called Muhleman Marketing, but I recommended on a sports call-in show on which Max was the guest that he change the name to Dream Makers, Inc. He

17

helped make my dream come true, and he was also influential in landing the new Carolina Panthers NFL franchise for Jerry Richardson and the people of Charlotte.

I'm in marketing, and I know how important it is to make a good impression. So each stage of our presentation for the NBA was designed to create a specific reaction. The video really helped them to understand why Charlotte was such a great market for basketball. There were aerial views of the coliseum under construction, along with graphs showing the popularity of basketball in North Carolina, the success of the Atlantic Coast Conference (ACC) teams, and demographics on the region we expected to draw from.

Some of the people at that meeting thought that Chapel Hill, where the University of North Carolina is located, was just a couple of miles away from Charlotte. They had no idea that the nearest ACC university is at least ninety minutes away and that the others are more than a two-hour drive. But when we showed them that we were right in the center of the entire region, they began to see how broad our drawing area would be.

> **Each stage of the presentation was designed to create a specific reaction.**

Two ACC teams, Georgia Tech and Clemson, are to the south of us, while Duke, Wake Forest, North Carolina, and NC State are to the north of us. Charlotte is right in the middle of basketball country, but the closest university is actually over a hundred miles away. That turned out to be a tremendous asset for us.

"The people of North Carolina are hungry for the sport they love," I told them, "and the message I bring to you from the people of Charlotte is simple: 'Bring the NBA to basketball country.'" That was our theme throughout the whole presentation, and I believe it made just the right impression.

Most of the men in that room had no idea how impressive our region truly is. After the video, I passed out our audited statements and financial reports, along with information on ticket sales, and then I ended by bringing out an oversized check for a million dollars—the money we'd already collected for season tickets—just to help make the point that we really meant business.

But the most oohs and aahs came when I told them I had already negotiated my lease with the city of Charlotte.

"This new coliseum that you have seen today is already being built," I said. "And our cost to lease it will be one dollar per game."

The room went wild. Some of the people stood up and applauded. Others made jokes or laughed out loud. The reason the lease made such a big impression was that it told them in no uncertain terms that we were serious. Suddenly every owner in the room was talking and laughing and saying what a great plan we had put together. One guy yelled out, "You're not getting a new team! I'm moving my team to Charlotte!" That was the exact response I had hoped for.

Of course, I didn't tell them any of the negatives. I wanted to present our situation in the most positive light possible. The fact is, several of the other teams already had better lease agreements than we did. While they may have paid more per game to lease their facilities, they were also getting a substantial portion of the concessions and parking receipts, which more than offset the difference. But just saying that we had landed a dollar-a-game lease made an outstanding impression on the people in the room, and now I believe that was what put us at the head of the pack.

Along with the comments about our lease agreement, we made sure that everything we submitted was prepared professionally and with enormous attention to detail. We had very capable, qualified lawyers. Our big-eight accounting firm had made sure that everything we submitted was audited and precise. It looked good, and it was clear that we weren't playing games. We made sure the owners and executives knew they could hang their hat on the information we were giving them, and that was what they wanted to see.

Not only did it tell them that our ownership group were all

19

good businessmen and negotiators, but they could see that the city of Charlotte was serious about getting a team. The people of North Carolina were behind us 100 percent.

"It's pretty clear that Mr. Shinn is working with a city that's behind him all the way, and they're going to help him," they said. For all the right reasons, we came off as winners.

When it was all over, we were thrilled with the way the meeting had gone. That was not the final decision day, however. We still had to go through a few more steps. And we weren't the first group or the last to make a presentation. Orlando went ahead of us, and they were in a bitter struggle with Miami to see who would be picked for a franchise. The word was that only one Florida city would have a shot at a franchise, and I understand that all the fireworks weren't at Walt Disney World that day. Apparently there were some later in that room.

If the deal had fallen through, I suspect I could have lost millions of dollars. I had already invested a lot of money in market studies, the promotional video, plane tickets, and other travel-related expenses, not to mention the cost of having Arthur Andersen on board. But when we flew home to North Carolina, my partners and I believed we had put our best foot forward. Ironically, to this day I don't remember everything that happened in the meeting. There was a lot of tension and the adrenaline was flowing, but when it was all over, Felix Sabates said, "The little guy slam-dunked 'em!" It was a good feeling, and to be truthful we were acting a little cocky. We were on top of the world. It didn't take long to get our attitudes adjusted.

In the exhilaration of the moment, someone suggested we change clothes and go play a round of golf. The adrenaline was still pumping, and that seemed like a good idea, so about an hour later four of us drove over to the golf club and signed in. As we waited for our tee time, we stood around laughing and joking and boasting about how well things had gone that morning. We felt so good after our success that we were sure everybody must know who we were. But when our turn to play came up, the starter called out the names over the loudspeaker: "The next group will be Mr. Mewlehan, Mr. Felix Sew-bates, and Mr. Shine." So much for our imaginary celebrity status! That brought us down to earth real fast.

Calculated Risks

Several weeks later I had to fly back to New York to make another presentation. We had finally come to the point where the league was going to tell us the price of the franchise, so things were getting more and more intense. If we were going to drop out, this would be the time. And to make things even more stressful, as the time approached to go up there, we began hearing rumors that the asking price was going to be higher than $25 million, which made us all a little nervous.

Felix Sabates has a Latin temper, and when we heard that the price might be going higher, he said, "I'm going with you. There ain't no way we're paying more than $25 million,

> **If we were going to drop out, this would be the time.**

and if those guys even mention it, I'm going to let them have it!" Well, you can imagine how that would have gone over with the league.

As luck would have it, Felix had to be at a conference in California on the day I was supposed to be at the league office. Before I went, he called my office and asked me to reschedule the meeting so he could take the red-eye from Los Angeles to New York and get there just in time for the presentation. If there was any change in the asking price, he was determined to play his trump card and give the expansion committee an earful.

In deference to Felix, I asked to be last or next to last to make my presentation, and the league agreed to my request. But when I talked to Felix on the phone, he said he was going to "cuss 'em out" if he had to and tell them we weren't going to pay a nickel more than $25 million. By that time I already knew the price was going to be more than that, and I realized

21

that we couldn't afford to have Felix there. If a shouting match erupted or if Felix "cussed 'em out" as he had promised, then all our hopes of getting a team would be shot.

So, just before I went to the airport, I called the NBA and told them that I needed to change my appointment one more time. If they would allow me, I'd like to have the first slot. They were gracious about it and called the city that was supposed to go first and asked if they would agree to flip-flop with me. They agreed, and I went to the meeting prepared to do whatever I had to do to stay in the running. But I didn't tell Felix anything about it, because I knew he wouldn't have taken the news kindly.

Later, the newspapers heard about my change of schedule and made a big deal out of it. That was the first Felix knew about what had really happened. He didn't get to cuss the NBA owners out, but he sure had a few words for me!

When I went in to the meeting to make the final presentation, the committee chairman didn't waste any time in telling me the price of the franchise. He just looked at me and said, "Mr. Shinn, the price is $32.5 million. Are you in or out?" I was a little surprised and not really prepared for that question, but I realized that if I hesitated or asked for more time to think it over, all our efforts could be lost. So I gulped and said, "We're in."

You can imagine the emotions that were running through my mind at that moment. Suddenly I had been hit with a 30 percent price hike, and one way or the other, I had to come up with another $7.5 million. Could I persuade the banks to go along with me? Would Rick, Felix, and Cy be willing to take the risk? Could I really pull it off? And if we did get the franchise, could we do all the things we were promising to do? I suppose I could have panicked and changed my mind on the spot, but I believed I was doing the right thing. And on top of everything else, I had already come so far. How could I turn back now?

My chief financial people had been with me for years, through numerous business ventures. Several had traveled with me to Los Angeles to take a look at the L.A. Express a couple of years earlier as a potential investment opportunity. These were trusted friends who had helped me make a fortune, but to a man, they tried to talk me out of going ahead with the NBA deal. Even before they knew the asking price was going to be so high, they told me, "George, if the price goes over $25 million, don't do it."

My mother-in-law told me, "George, you'd have to be crazy to pay that much money for a basketball team. You've worked so hard to get where you are, and you are finally in a position to take care of my daughter and grandchildren in a decent way. If you go through with this deal, you're going to blow it!"

I was getting hit from all sides. Charles Ricks, who had been my key adviser over all the years, said, "George, don't do this." Charles had been with the Carolina Cougars back during the ABA days, and he watched them go under. He recog-

> *In the end, I knew I had to trust my heart. I had to go for it.*

nized the risks involved, and he didn't want me getting in over my head.

I prayed over the thing. I thought about it and listened to everybody's input. But in the end, I knew I had to trust my heart. Whether you call it intuition, God's intervention, or just my blockheaded stubbornness, I couldn't give up. I had to go for it. I sat down with Charles one day and talked it over, trying to come to some sort of agreement.

"Charles," I said, "you are one of the most brilliant accountants in this state, and I respect your opinion a lot. I understand your point of view, and I know why you have recommended that I don't go ahead with this plan. I believe it will work and I'm going to do it anyway. But, Charles," I said, "I don't want you to quit on me. Stay with me and help me through this thing. I'm going to do it, and I need your help."

Today, Charles just laughs about that conversation. Obviously, the Hornets are becoming one of the hottest franchises in the NBA, and we have been very successful in every way. One day, after the deals were all signed and we were on our way up the charts, Charles told me, "Well, George, that's why you're the entrepreneur and I'm the accountant!"

In the spring of 1988 I was notified by the NBA that the expansion committee was going to be meeting on April 1, and they were going to make their final decision on the expansion teams at that time.

I thought that was an interesting time for them to meet. Yes, it was April Fools' Day, and I suppose I could easily have felt like a fool if things had not turned out the way they did. But the first of April has always been a special day for me. For one thing, it's my wedding anniversary. So I said to myself, "Well, they're going to make the decision on my special day. Maybe something good is going to happen." Then I just held my breath.

Welcome to the NBA

On the morning of April 1, I went in to the office early. I wanted to be there when the phone rang, no matter what time of day the call came in. When the call didn't come that morning, I had lunch brought in and ate at my desk. I waited by the phone until about seven o'clock that night. It never rang. At one point I called the NBA office and asked if the expansion committee was still meeting, and David Stern's secretary told me they were. Finally I went home, totally drained, afraid to find out the bad news.

I can't remember ever feeling so disappointed and depressed. When I got home, I pulled into the garage and just sat there in the car. I said to myself, "I'm out of it. They haven't called because they don't want me. The newspapers and the critics were right. We never had a chance, and all the time and effort and money I've spent for all these months has been wasted."

When I finally worked up the energy to go into the house, my oldest son, Chris, met me at the door. He said, "Dad, you just got a call from David Stern, and he wants you to call him back." I was so low I was practically crawling on the floor, and I didn't show any emotion at all. So Chris said, louder this time, "Dad! David Stern is the commissioner of the NBA, and he just called you!"

I said, "Son, I know who David Stern is. I'll call him in a few minutes." I thought about it for a minute, and realizing that I was going to get the worst news of my life, I decided I was not about to call him from the den, where the whole family could see me break down. If the conversation went the way I expected, I didn't want them to see me cry when Stern gave me the bad news. So I went to the master bedroom and took the phone on into the bathroom to call from there.

I was so nervous I dialed the wrong number the first time and had to re-dial. That only increased my anxiety. This time when the receptionist answered, I told her who I was and that I was returning Mr. Stern's call. She said, "Hold on, Mr. Shinn."

> **I was so nervous I dialed the wrong number the first time and had to redial.**

It seemed like forever before David Stern came on the line. When he did, he was very straightforward. He said, "George, this is April Fools' Day, but what I'm about to tell you is not an April Fools' joke. I'm calling you first because you were picked first." He paused, and then he added, "Welcome to the NBA!"

I couldn't believe my ears. I was so excited I couldn't even speak. I stared at my reflection in the mirror in disbelief until Stern said, "George, are you there?"

"Yes, David," I laughed, with tears in my eyes. "I'm here. I'm just so happy and so excited I don't know what to say!"

Suddenly it began to sink in that I hadn't lost the franchise at all, but we were the league's *first choice* of an expansion city.

I nearly went through the roof. When I told my family what had happened, they were laughing and jumping up and down, almost as excited as I was. The next thing I did was to jump in my car and drive over to Max Muhleman's house to tell him the good news. His video and marketing materials had been a big part of our success, and I wanted him to be among the first to know. We laughed and hugged and cried in his kitchen.

David Stern had warned me, "George, you know you can't tell a soul about this until we make the official press announcement from the NBA offices in New York." David had said that I could tell our investment group and our closest supporters, but there had to be absolute secrecy. If the news leaked out before the official announcement, it could jeopardize the deal. No one but the National Basketball Association could make an official announcement like that, and that wouldn't be done until the next day.

But we celebrated among ourselves, and the next day we all went down to the old coliseum and talked and celebrated some more and compared notes on what was going to happen. It was an absolutely wonderful time; none of us will ever forget it.

As soon as the NBA made their announcement to the media, the inquiries started coming. Our phones were ringing off the hook, and reporters were all over the place. We scheduled a press conference to be attended by Mayor Gantt and many of the dignitaries of Charlotte, and of course, that added to the excitement.

The main thing that I wanted people to know, and that nobody had mentioned up to that point, was that we were picked first. What made that so special for me was that, from the very beginning, we were always picked to finish last. In every poll, in every column, and in every article written about us, we were last. Nobody put us anywhere near the top, let alone first, but here we were! Me, the kid who had finished at the bottom of his class. I just wanted the world to know that not only did we make it but we were first!

3

It's a Matter of Believing

SOME people call it the school of hard knocks. I call it life as usual. We don't get to choose the kind of life we get when we start out. Life comes to us on its own terms, and one way or another we learn to cope with it. Growing up in Kannapolis, about twenty-five miles north of Charlotte, I watched a lot of my friends just settle into life the easiest way they could. No matter how hard their situation might have been, they simply accepted what they got and held on for the ride. That was certainly the way I started out, but along the way there were to be some dramatic changes in my circumstances.

My earliest memories are of life on our family's farm. It was a good life in the beginning, but about as far from the NBA and the media spotlight as you could ever imagine. We were fairly comfortable, with plenty of work, lots of time to play, and more than enough to eat. My father owned and operated a small service station and grocery store across the road from our house. In some ways it was like the convenience stores we have today, where you can buy gas and groceries and certain kinds of household items. He worked there every day except Sunday, and he made a good living for us.

My father had three children from a previous marriage and my mother had one when I came on the scene. I was the baby of the family and their only child together.

We had a small farm where we raised a few crops and had a few farm animals. I helped out as much as I could at that age, but I didn't have too many worries in the early days. I went fishing and played with my pals. We wrestled in the haystacks and teased the girls, until I eventually entered public school and began playing organized sports. It was a busy life, and there were always lots of people coming and going around our place.

But when I was eight years old, my father died, and the peace and comfort of my childhood began to slip away little by little. There were three children still at home in the beginning. But as things grew more and more difficult, my fifteen-year-old sister got married and left the nest. My brother joined the air force at eighteen. Eventually they all left, and my mother and I were left to run what was left of the family business.

Things continued to get worse. My mother had been a good homemaker, but she simply didn't have a head for business. She couldn't keep track of the financial details like my father did, and whenever neighbors couldn't afford to pay their bills, she didn't have the heart to put pressure on them. When it became apparent that we were not going to be able to make a go of it, my mother was forced to close down the station and the store, and eventually she had to auction off the farm and most of our possessions.

I can remember very vividly—at the age of nine—watching the people coming in to bid on the service station and our land. The only thing my mother was trying to keep was our house. She made an opening bid, and some people we didn't know started bidding against her. Obviously they didn't know she was trying to save the house and our last bit of dignity. But somebody told them, and when they found out what was happening, they came over and apologized to my mother and said they hadn't realized our situation. So she ended up getting to keep the house and a little bit of property. From that moment on, life was very hard.

Swallowing Hard

From having a pretty good life, I suddenly found out what it was like to go hungry and not to be able to buy nice clothes or even the most basic things I had once taken for granted. I learned to say thank you to people who gave me a hand-me-down jacket or a pair of shoes. And through the assistance of the county welfare department, I was able to get free lunches at school, which was another experience that took some getting used to. They were lean years, and despite some happy moments, it was a time of stress and strain that would have a lasting impact upon my life and my outlook.

> *I suddenly found out what it was like to go hungry and not to be able to buy even the most basic things.*

The incident that had perhaps the most profound effect on me at that time happened when I was in the fifth grade. Like a lot of boys at the age of ten or eleven, I had a special little girlfriend, one particular girl in my class who was special to me.

She was pretty, smart, and everybody knew she was the leader of the class. She was the best reader, the quickest learner, and among other things, she was the one who collected the lunch money when it was time to eat. On one particular day we got into some kind of minor disagreement about something or other I can't recall. We were still friends, but she was angry and wanted to get even, as I would soon find out. At that time there was another girl in the class who everybody knew was extremely poor. She had a pretty bad reputation, she came to school unwashed, and the kids teased her a lot. There was even a story that some of the teachers had to wash her up before school so she could come to class.

Each day, my little girlfriend was supposed to go around and collect the lunch money before we went to the cafeteria to eat, and on this particular day the teacher asked her if everyone had paid. So, glancing at me, she announced to the class that there were twenty-eight paid lunches and two *free* lunches, and then she called out our names. It was the first time she had ever said it just that way. She did it to make me mad, but it didn't. Instead, it hurt me deeply.

I had a lot of pride and didn't want everybody to know that my family was having trouble. But you know, when I look back now, I thank God that it happened that way, because that experience planted the seed in my mind that would one day set me on a course to turn things around. That one moment of humiliation, as innocent as it was, compelled me to find some way to turn my adversity into an advantage and to turn my tough times into opportunities.

Somehow, some way, in my heart of hearts, I made myself a vow at that precise moment that I would never again go through that kind of embarrassment. I decided I would scale whatever walls got in the way and go around the ones I couldn't climb. Whatever it took, I would find some way to keep from being hurt again. Today, whenever I think about those times and remember the experiences that molded my thinking and turned me around, I think first of that defining moment in the fifth grade. Isn't it amazing how such a little thing could have such a lasting impact?

There are so many kids today who have so much, but they complain that they don't have enough. A lot of people seem to think that the best way to take care of their kids is to give them everything they want and never deny them anything so they can be *somebody.* But, more often than not, it's the hard times and the adversities that give young people the experiences that will push them out of their complacency and force them to do something with their lives. That's certainly the way it worked in my case. I think it's tragic that an entire generation of young Americans has been deprived of those hard-won experiences by parents, relatives, and even educators who think they're supposed to give them everything.

One of the results of my experience was that it gave me a better understanding and a lasting concern for the problems that people from disadvantaged backgrounds have to deal with. When I got involved in the proprietary-school business many years later, I was able to reach out to all kinds of people who wanted to change their circumstances and make a new life for themselves. I was especially interested in working with students who were underprivileged, whether it was economically, academically, socially, or whatever.

The bad things that happened to me as a child actually ended up helping me in my quest to help others. I became an advocate for various kinds of educational and social reform. I wanted to be part of changing the circumstances that were holding people back. I wanted to show them that with a little determination and a positive attitude they could open themselves up to all sorts of new opportunities.

The Problem with School
Had it not been for sports, I'm not sure I would have finished high school at all.

I was a fun-loving kid in school, and I liked hanging around with my friends, pulling pranks on people, and most of all, playing baseball. The last thing on my mind was doing homework. When I got home from school each day, I wanted to go out and shoot baskets, scare up a game of sandlot ball, or do anything else I could do outdoors instead of going inside to study. I didn't have the patience or the inclination

31

for academics, and it would be years before I realized what problems that would eventually create for me.

Now, I don't want to suggest that I was some kind of great athlete or anything, because that was not the case. But I was an *eager* athlete, and I loved baseball and track and the whole sports environment. What I lacked in skill I made up for in determination. Like a lot of people who are small in stature, I was fast on my feet. At five-foot-six, I wasn't going to be a power forward or a linebacker on anybody's team, but I was quick, persistent, and hard to shake loose when I got hold of somebody. The truth be known, that's probably what kept me in school.

When I speak to young people today at high schools and public events of various kinds, I generally encourage them to balance their outside interests and their schoolwork. To be a well-rounded person, you need a certain amount of recreational activity and a certain amount of scholarship. Too much of either one makes you less than a whole person. But I also tell them it's never too late to make a fresh start and to put things back into balance. In my business schools, I always told new students, "Whatever you did or didn't do in school, put it behind you now. That's where it belongs. Because this is a new day."

> **I don't remember ever reading a book when I was in school.**

I don't remember ever reading a book from cover to cover when I was in school. It wasn't until I was in business college that I finally read a book all the way through, and the experience was life-changing. I had no idea how exciting a good book could be or how challenging it is to wrestle with ideas and concepts in books.

The incident that perhaps best indicates just how lazy I was as a student happened in my senior year in high school. As I said, I wasn't interested in reading books of any kind when I was in school. If I could read the stuff on the back of the book, or maybe the first and last chapter, and get some vague idea of what the book was about, I thought that should be enough. But, as I was to discover, it didn't work that way.

I had to write a report, so I asked a friend of mine if he had ever read a book, and he said he had. He told me all about it and related some of the important incidents I could use in my report. After listening to his account, I went back to my room and wrote a paper to turn in the next day. Unfortunately, it didn't take the teacher long to figure out what I had done.

She called me up after class and said, "George, I must say, you did a good job writing up your report, but I know you didn't read the book." She handed back the paper, and in the very first sentence she had marked through the word *Silver* and written in *Civil*. The book I was supposed to have read was about the Civil War, and I didn't even know enough about it to spell the name correctly. I had called it the Silver War. My teacher had a pretty good idea that I didn't know what I was talking about.

Talk about embarrassed! How could I have been such a dummy? Fortunately, that was toward the end of my senior year, and I didn't have to write any more papers that year! You know, we all make mistakes, and hopefully we learn from those mistakes. That one taught me a lesson I will never forget. To cheat, to copy, to borrow someone else's idea is dishonest, and it is irresponsible. I can't say I was a changed person after that experience, but I began to see just how important it is to do your own work and take your assignments seriously.

My class graduated from high school in 1959, but I was not eligible to graduate with them because I had to take two courses in summer school. So while my classmates were all crossing the stage, I was out having fun at the beach. And when I was finally allowed to graduate, I got my diploma in the mail. In fact, the first graduation I ever attended came much later when I attended the commencement exercises at Owensboro Business College in Owensboro, Kentucky, and I was the guest speaker.

After I picked up my high school diploma at the end of the summer, I went to work in the mill. It wasn't until much later, when I enrolled in business school and studied accounting and principles of business, that I began to develop a desire to learn. At one point I read everything I could get my hands on, and I would jump from one book to the next because I had finally discovered the sheer excitement of learning.

I'm sorry now that I didn't discover it sooner. Today, I'm able to use my own example to encourage young people to reach beyond themselves and tap into all those wonderful treasures that can make their lives fuller and richer.

> *Today I try to get the point across to kids that the important thing is not that you graduate first in your class, but that you graduate.*

It is ironic that even though I never read a book from cover to cover when I was in school, I have ended up writing five books of my own. Life is full of surprises, and I've known my share.

Incentives for Learning

Today, I believe that a teacher's most important task is to help students discover the value of knowledge and to make them want to learn. You can't teach unless your students want to learn. You can't stuff it in their heads; they've got to open up and accept it for themselves. That's the only way it can have any lasting effect on them.

College never entered my mind when I was in school. If I had considered the possibility, even for a moment, I'm sure my teachers would have told me to forget it. But it didn't happen. I hated to study, and going to college or university so I could study some more was not in my plans! The only reason I graduated from high school in the first place was because I had a mom who wouldn't give up on me. She was determined to see her little boy graduate from school, and she made me promise I'd do that . . . a promise I often regretted making!

There was, however, one other factor. By the time I was old enough to drive a car, my mother had bought an old 1951 Chevrolet, and like most teenagers, I couldn't wait to get my hands on it. But my mother was clever, and the only way she would let me use the car was if I accomplished certain goals she had set for me. For one thing, she made me promise that I wouldn't smoke or drink until I was out of school. If I did either of those things, I would lose my car privileges. And since she wanted me to graduate more than anything else, she made me promise to stay in school and do whatever I had to do to get my diploma.

I am glad to say I honored my commitment—barely—and finally made it. I didn't cross the stage with my class, but I did receive my diploma, and that made my mother very happy. Today I try to get the point across to kids that the important thing is not that you graduate first in your class, but that you graduate.

On May 30, 1977, I had the privilege of being inducted into the A. L. Brown High School Hall of Fame. What makes that honor so unusual is that that's the high school I graduated from in Kannapolis. I had not been a good student when I was in high school, but I had learned a lot since that time. Later, in 1994, I was invited back as the keynote speaker at the opening activities for all faculty and staff of Kannapolis city schools. It was an honor I will not soon forget.

I was introduced by the superintendent of schools, a gentleman named Ed Tyson. Dr. Tyson introduced me and explained why it was important that I come back to speak to the people of Kannapolis.

He doesn't go by Eddie anymore, but that's how I remember Dr. Tyson. We grew up together and graduated in the same high school class. Eddie was an outstanding scholar, and he went on to college after we finished school and earned a master's degree and doctorate, and then entered the field of education. Along the way he married one of the prettiest girls in our high school class and had a distinguished teaching career. I couldn't help thinking about how ironic it was that, more than thirty years later, we were there together on that stage: Eddie, the smartest kid in school, and me, the boy least likely to succeed.

They were having some problems at Brown High School when Dr. Tyson invited me to speak. There had been some unrest and classroom disturbances. People around there were feeling pretty tense. The press made a big issue out of it—bigger than it actually was as it turns out—and when I saw the reports in the newspapers, I called Ed and asked if there was anything I could do to help. I suggested that one or two of the Charlotte Hornets might be willing to come with me, and we would be happy to offer some encouragement.

He was glad to have the help. He asked if I would come back and help start a second-chance program for kids who were underachievers—that is, kids like me. Some of those young people were constantly getting into trouble, they were academically weak, and many came from single-parent or no-parent families. For whatever reasons, these were the kids who always caused problems and were in danger of being tossed out of school.

Over a period of time I endowed and helped launch the George Shinn Alternative School. My initial contribution got the program started, and today I help the school put on an annual golf tournament to raise the money to keep it going. Not everybody can be a top performer, but everybody deserves a chance to succeed. It has been a wonderful privilege for me to be involved with this program, and every time I go there it reminds me that there is no life so far gone that it cannot be turned around. After all, I am living proof.

Stand and Be Recognized

At the 1977 awards ceremony, certificates and awards were presented to students who had peformed at a high level in academics and sports during the school year. During the presentations, I noticed that it seemed to be the same dozen or so kids who were winning all the awards. They were the brightest or the most industrious, and time after time, they kept going back for more awards. When I went up to the platform to speak, I looked out across all the other students in that room who had not won any awards. They deserved to be recognized too, because they had come to school every day and done their best. Even if they weren't winning the awards, they were important.

As I began my remarks, I said, "We're certainly proud of these students who have worked so hard and won all these awards, but I see a lot of others out there who didn't win any awards today. I want to say that *you* all deserve credit too. You should all be recognized because you've been in school for twelve years, and you have worked hard to get to this point. Even if you didn't get a certificate today, I think you are special. I would like all those students who did not receive an award today to stand up and be recognized." At that point, not only did those students stand up, but the whole audience rose to its feet and cheered and applauded. They understood my message. Every student in that room was special, and somebody needed to say so.

> *Every student in that room was special, and somebody needed to say so.*

When I went in 1994 to speak to the faculty and staff of the Kannapolis city schools, I asked Gil McGregor, who is the color commentator for the Charlotte Hornets basketball games on television, to come with me. Gil is a former player in the NBA and before that was one of the outstanding players at Wake Forest University. He stands about six-foot-eight and weighs around three hundred pounds. He was a big hit with the teachers and administrators alike. When we came up to the stage together, Dr. Tyson introduced us as the center and the point guard—there was no question who was who!

I said, "Thank you, Dr. Tyson. It is a real pleasure for me to come back to my old school, especially when the guy who finished last in his class can be introduced by the guy who finished first." Eddie told me later he didn't actually graduate first—maybe the actual valedictorian was that little girl who embarrassed me back in the fifth grade!—but that was the quote that appeared in the local newspaper the next day.

The opportunities to go back and speak at my old school were a privilege I can hardly describe. When I was going to school, I had no idea that I would ever have the opportunity to speak before a group of teachers and try to motivate people who were once classmates of mine. There was even one teacher still there who had been teaching at Brown in my day. There's no telling what kind of stories she could have told about me!

The message I take to places like that today is simple but often overlooked. I tell them that people are generally helpful if you're courteous and if you thank them for their help. But you have to be willing to ask for help when you need it. If you're too proud to admit that you need a hand or if you act like you don't want their help, then you probably won't get it. I learned early on that if you let people know when you need help and show them that you appreciate it, most people are generous enough to try to help you out.

On the other side of the coin, if you extend a helping hand to people who need it, then you are helping to build faith and trust in people, and in ways you may not recognize at the time, you are even contributing to the strength and vitality of our nation. When you help one person, you help everybody.

I never had much in the way of financial resources as a youngster, but I learned a very important lesson from my mother. She used to say that if I had faith, God would be there for me to help make things better. Even if I didn't fully comprehend what she meant by that in the beginning, I remembered her words later on, and they helped get me through a lot of tough situations.

Mother would say, "Someday, George, you're going to find yourself in a tough situation, and you're going to need God's help. Whether it's in school, or work, or in some other part of your life, you're going to need him. When you find yourself in trouble, just remember, if you have faith, God has the power." Over the past twenty years or so, I have discovered time and time again how wise those words really were. Those principles have guided me in my business and everything else I have done.

4

Going against the Odds

WHEN I was very young, I had a problem with stuttering and stammering. In fact, I was petrified to speak in front of people, and the prospect of giving an oral report in school would almost make me comatose. I would much rather take a zero or fail the course than stand up in front of the class and give a speech.

In those days, the teacher would go down the roll and call on each student in alphabetical order to read a sentence or two from the book. That was a fairly common practice in a lot of schools. When she got to me, I would always freeze up. I couldn't read out loud. To cover up for my embarrassment,

I would pretend that I couldn't keep up or that I had lost my place and didn't know where we were.

The truth was, I just couldn't get the words to come out. You can imagine what a humiliating feeling that was, and one of the main reasons I hated school so much was this fear of reading out loud.

But one day I got a teacher who could see that something unusual was going on with me. She decided she was going to try to help. I'll never forget her. Her name was Mrs. Drummond, and her husband was the principal of our school. Not only was she a very nice lady, she was also an excellent teacher. She stopped me after class one day and said, "George, what's going on? Why don't you pay attention during our reading lesson? Why is it that every time I call on you, you won't respond?"

My lip started to quiver a little and I looked down in embarrassment. "I can't," I said.

She put her hand on my shoulder to reassure me. "What do you mean you can't, George? Don't you know how to read?"

"Yes, ma'am," I said, "I can read. But I'm scared to read in front of the whole class."

"Oh, I see." She thought about it for a minute, then said she wanted to help me, and she asked, "Is there any time when it would be better for me to call on you during our reading time?"

"Yes," I said. "If you called on me first, I think I could do it. When you start going down the line and I know I'm going to be fifth or tenth, I start thinking about it, and I get too nervous to talk. But I probably wouldn't be too scared if I was the first one."

"All right, then," she said, "the next time we have a reading

> *From that day on I knew I wasn't going to be embarrassed in front of the class, and little by little I overcame my fear of speaking in front of people.*

lesson, I'm going to call on you first. If I see that you're having a problem, then I'll just call on somebody else. Would that be all right with you?" It was a wonderful plan, and I told her I'd like to try it. Well, that really helped me calm down. From that day on I knew I wasn't going to be embarrassed in front of the class, and little by little I overcame my fear of speaking in front of people.

The concern and personal attention of that one teacher was a godsend for me. Here was a woman who had the insight and the foresight to care about one little boy who was frightened half to death, and her personal concern made a lasting impression on me. As a result, when I wound up in the proprietary-school business later on, I tried to find ways to show the same kind of concern for my students, and I encouraged my instructors to look for ways to help their students solve their learning problems with the same kind of creativity and compassion.

Today, I'm convinced that our phenomenal success in the school business was due, at least in part, to that principle. Over the years, that one simple lesson I learned from Mrs. Drummond has helped hundreds, even thousands, of young people to deal with their problems and to earn a business school diploma. The moral is that sometimes one good deed can have an impact far beyond the scope of the incident in which it first occurred.

Going On, Moving Up

After I finished high school I went to work where I thought I'd spend the rest of my life—in the textile plant. I had just turned eighteen, and they couldn't put me on the night shift until I was nineteen. So I started off on the first shift at Cannon Mills. Had they left me there, I would probably still be working in Kannapolis to this day. But for some reason they decided to move some of us around, and I was moved to the second shift.

Now the second shift is from three in the afternoon to eleven at night. It may be a good shift for some people, but it was a terrible shift for a young man like me who was full of energy and looking for a good time. I was eighteen years old, after all, full of vinegar, and the afternoon shift was just killing my social life.

Three till eleven was the time kids my age wanted to be out doing things and seeing people, so it wasn't long before I went back to management and asked to be moved to the first shift. They said they couldn't do that, but they would agree to transfer me to another department and put me on the third shift, which was from eleven at night to seven in the morning. That meant I would have most of my day available and the afternoon as well. I didn't mind working the night shift, so I accepted the new assignment.

They put me in what they called the bleachery, and I spent most of my shift lifting great big rolls of cloth that had just been woven. The rolls of new fabric were transported through the bleach, through a wash and rinse cycle, and the new cloth came out a clean, natural color. But the rolls were huge and very heavy, and before long I started having severe back pains. I wound up going from one doctor to another, trying to get some relief.

For the first time in my life I realized I needed an education.

I went through treatments of every conceivable kind without success. None of the doctors I went to could tell me exactly what the problem was. One guy said I had one leg shorter than the other. Another decided I had arthritis, and some of them started telling me about diseases and conditions I couldn't begin to pronounce. Well, all that bad news wasn't doing much for my peace of mind or my job performance.

After watching me go month after month, switching from one treatment to another, one of my friends told me to stop going to all those quacks and make an appointment with an orthopedic surgeon, who could tell me what was really wrong with me. That's what I did, and after a thorough exam-

44

ination the specialist told me I had chronic back strain due to a genetic curvature of the spine. It wasn't particularly severe or dangerous, he said, but it was the root cause of my back pains, and if I continued lifting those heavy rolls of cloth, it would lead to permanent spinal injuries and a lifetime of disability.

That was enough for me. It led to some pretty major changes in my life. It wasn't good news, but that pain in my back was the first thing that ever made me start thinking seriously about going back to school. For the first time in my life I realized I needed an education.

I decided that what I wanted to do was go to the local business school and learn some basic skills so I could get a job in the office at the textile plant. At the same time, I set myself a goal of earning $100 a week. That would have been a big-time salary for a boy my age in those days, but that was my target. I believed I could do it if I got a good job at the plant. I had a lot of spunk, and I believed I could work my way up the ladder. And that was probably the first indication that there may have been some entrepreneurial spirit in me.

Changing Directions

When I enrolled at Evans Business College in Concord, North Carolina, I had no idea what a major step in my life it would turn out to be.

My high school friend, Glenn Compton, enrolled at Evans at the same time I did, and we went to classes together. We must have looked like the odd couple. Glenn was the three-hundred-pound tackle and I was the little running back, but we were stuck together like glue. We had been pals for many years, and we were good for each other. He was the big strong guy; I was the little, loud crazy guy. We were generally on the same wavelength, and we remained best friends for many years.

Glenn introduced me to the writer Ian Fleming, the author of all those James Bond books. I started with the first one, *On*

Her Majesty's Secret Service, and when I finished it, I was shocked to realize what all I had been missing. Suddenly I was upset that it took me all those years to discover how much enjoyment there was in reading a good book. I loved it! I started reading all the Ian Fleming books I could get my hands on. This was during the time that the James Bond films were becoming popular at the movies, so that made the experience all the more interesting for me.

That was also the time that some of our teachers were introducing us to the classic works of self-help and motivational literature. Among them were such books as *Think and Grow Rich* by Napoleon Hill and *The Power of Positive Thinking* by Norman Vincent Peale. Those books had a profound impact on my thinking, and they helped me discover that I had more control over my life than I had ever imagined.

I didn't just read those books; I devoured them. I memorized them, underlined key passages, and studied them until I knew the principles of success backward and forward. I used to write out slogans on slips of paper and tack them up on the walls of my room. I put them there to help keep me motivated and to stimulate me to do my best. It must have worked, because I began taking a serious interest in all my subjects and poured myself into my schoolwork.

During this time, it wasn't at all uncommon for the faculty or staff members at the school to ask students for leads on other potential students. One day, one of the recruiters on campus came up to me and asked if I knew anyone who might be interested in coming to Evans Business College. I said, "Sure, I probably know at least a hundred."

His eyes lit up. That was the best news he'd heard all day. He pulled out his pad and pencil and asked me for some of those names and numbers. Well, this was business school, and I had been learning my lessons from some of the best, so I said, "No problem. I'll give you as many as you like for ten dollars apiece."

He backed up and looked at me like I was some sort of space alien. "What?" he said. "You mean you would do that to your own school!"

I said, "Sure I would. You're charging me to go to school here, aren't you, and I have to make a living just like you do!"

"Hmm," he grunted. "I see what you mean. Well, maybe we can work something out." Later that week he talked to the school owner. When he came back to see me, he said the director wasn't willing to pay me cash for my leads, but they would give me credit toward my tuition for all the leads I could develop. That sounded like a fair bargain, so I started giving them leads that helped pay my way through school.

Cleaning Up

Prior to that time I had difficulty finding a job that would pay enough and also let me work in the morning or evening so that I could attend classes during the day. As I looked around the area, I found out that the local bakery used young men to load the trucks early in the morning, and I decided that would be a good place to apply. When I went in, the foreman told me he needed another person but couldn't afford to hire anybody else at the moment.

> *"I just wanted to show you I could do the work. If I do a good job, you can pay me. If I don't, you don't need to pay me a dime."*

I thought about that all day, and the next morning at five o'clock I showed up at the bakery. I hadn't been hired; I just went out on the dock and started pushing loaded boxes of bread onto the trucks. One of the guys working there came over and asked me, "When did you start to work here?"

"Today's my first day," I said. I didn't tell him I hadn't been hired. I worked all that day and the next before anybody in management realized they had an extra man on the dock. On the third day one of the bosses came up and said, "What

47

are you doing working out here? You haven't even been hired!"

I said, "I know, but I need the job, and I just wanted to show you I could do the work. If I do a good job, you can pay me. If I don't, you don't need to pay me a dime." He shook his head and I went back to work. At the end of the week I got a paycheck, and they gave me a job. I wouldn't necessarily recommend that everybody try that, but it worked for me at a time when I really needed it.

As much as that job helped me make ends meet, it wasn't long before I realized that I still needed more money for tuition, clothes, and books than I could make working at the bakery. So I went and talked to the administrators at the school again. I told them my problem, and they gave me a job at the business college as a part-time janitor. As payment I would receive free tuition.

There was a regular janitorial crew at the school that took care of most of the major stuff, waxing and buffing floors and things of that sort, but I would sweep up the classrooms, arrange the chairs, dust the erasers, take out the trash, and other things that helped keep the place looking neat. I also had to restock the bathrooms and clean the toilets. Being a part-time janitor wasn't so bad, and it also kept me around the school instead of someplace else that had nothing to do with the learning environment.

I was dating another student at the school at that time, the young woman who would later become my wife. On Saturdays I would drive up to the school, make my janitorial rounds, then clean myself up in the bathroom, change clothes, and go see Carolyn. I hurried to get through with my job as early as possible so we could go out, but once in a while I was delayed, and Carolyn would have to wait for me.

When Opportunity Knocks

That's exactly what happened one Saturday when I had finished my duties and was about to leave. I had gotten all cleaned up, put on fresh clothes, splashed on some cologne, and was just about to leave when two cute girls came up to the front door. There wasn't anyone else around to help them, so I unlocked the door and said, "Hello, can I help you?"

They said, "Hi! Do you work here?"

I said, "Yes, I do." I didn't tell them that I was the janitor, but I didn't lie, either. They were attractive girls, just a couple of years younger than I was, and I thought it would be all right if they were a little bit impressed with me.

They said, "We're interested in enrolling in your school. Could you show us around?"

By this time I was feeling a little cocky, I suppose, so I introduced myself as Mr. Shinn and said, "Sure, I'd be happy to." Of course, I had all the keys to the classrooms, offices, closets, and supply rooms—a janitor has to be able to get in and out. For all they knew I could have been a teacher or recruiter. I didn't have a business card to offer them, but I smiled a lot, showed them around, and made sure they saw all the best stuff.

I knew where everything was because I was a student myself. I knew all about the typewriters and adding machines and the course materials we used. I knew about all the business systems and textbooks and how classes were set up and scheduled. In short, I knew everything they needed to know.

After the tour, I took them back up to the front office, gave them catalogs and application forms, and did my best to convince them that enrolling at Evans Business College would be the best decision they could ever make. After half an hour or so they left, and I hurried off to pick up Carolyn. And I promptly forgot all about those unexpected visitors.

The following Monday, however, the girls came back, accompanied by two of their friends. They had all filled out applications to enroll, and they came to the front office and told the receptionist they wanted to speak to Mr. Shinn. They were holding the application forms, and it was obvious they intended to enroll, but they insisted on seeing me first.

The receptionist paused for a minute, trying to figure out

what in the world was going on, and just to make sure she had heard them correctly, she said, "Did you mean George Shinn?"

"Yes," they said. "He works here, doesn't he?"

"Oh yes," the receptionist answered. "Yes, he works here."

"Then we'd like to see him. We have our applications ready, but we won't give them to anybody but Mr. Shinn."

"I see," she answered. "If you'll wait just a minute, I'll check to see if Mr. Shinn is in today," and she went back to the director's office and told him what was going on.

A few minutes later the director came up to my room and got me out of class. He said, "George, this is a little bit unusual, but we've got some prospective new students down here who apparently talked to you Saturday about enrolling at Evans Business College. One of them says you gave her a tour of the school."

Was it an accident? I can't help but think that God had already planned that situation to happen just the way it did.

"Sure," I said. "I remember. Two girls came by Saturday afternoon and they wanted to know about enrolling in the school, so I showed them around."

"Well, they have come back," he said, "only this time they brought a couple more friends with them, and they *all* want to enroll. They have their application forms all filled out, and they're ready to sign up—but they say they're not going to give those applications to anybody but you."

Needless to say, my stock went up around Evans Business College! I went down and accepted the applications and welcomed four new students to our school. I laid it on a little thick and asked them if they had any more friends I could talk to about the school, and one thing led to another. To make a long story short, as a result of that little episode I got a full-time job as a recruiter for the school.

That's the true story of how I got involved in the school business. Was it an accident? I can't help but think that God had already planned that situation to happen just the way it did. I didn't lie to the girls; I did work there. I simply used some charm and salesmanship, and it paid off in a very special way.

That experience was an important object lesson for me, as well, because it let me know that I had some talents, perhaps some charm, and it helped me to start focusing on the areas where my talents really lay. The school already had two full-time recruiters when I started my new job. But by the time the next start date came around, I had enrolled more students by myself than both of the professionally trained recruiters combined. The owner at that time had two schools, and before long I wound up taking over all the recruiting duties for both schools. That's how my career as an entrepreneur got started.

When Good Things Happen

"Being at the right place at the right time." How many times have you heard that expression? That's all it was, but it opened the door for me. The lesson was that I wasn't lying around, moaning about being broke or wishing something good would happen in my life. I was working, paying my bills, and doing the best I could to get ahead.

From that one experience I learned that luck never comes to people who are content to sit around and wait for their big break. Nobody becomes successful because they deserve it. If you want to be at the right place, at the right time, you've got to put yourself in motion, do what you know how to do, and do it with conviction. Then one day when you are at the right place, and the right time just happens to roll around, you'll be ready. From my own personal experience, I am convinced that this is the main way good things happen.

51

Obviously that experience helped me a lot. It gave me confidence and faith—in myself and in God. In some ways, I would even compare the experience to what happened at the start of the 1994–95 basketball season, when it looked as if we had a good chance of bringing in one of the two outstanding free agents available that summer. We were very interested in getting Danny Manning or Horace Grant to play for us, and we believed that both of them wanted to play for the Hornets. We negotiated in good faith, made hard offers that were at the top of the range for the young talent coming into the league, and tried to bring the players and their agents to Charlotte so they could get a feel for our club. I felt good about the way we handled things.

In the end, we didn't get either of those players. Everybody recognizes that it was a complicated situation; but in my heart of hearts I believe the right thing happened. I believe the way things worked out was the right thing for the Charlotte Hornets at that moment. We took a roasting from the media during all that business, and there were some hard feelings on both sides. But when all is said and done, I am convinced we will see that the right thing happened after all. I was doing everything I knew how to do at the time. I took the ethical position and followed all the rules. And even though I was trying very hard to get either one of those players, things took off in a direction of their own. Time will tell, but I suspect we were not meant to get those players.

The lesson is this: As long as you keep doing what's right and try to conduct your affairs honorably and ethically, I truly believe that right and good will prevail. The best results come from hard work, solid planning, honest motives, and whatever else you can do to bring about the desired results.

There is an old saying that if you try to open one door and it simply won't open, then move on to the next door and try again. I believe that is a great principle, and I have applied it countless times in my life. Sometimes, when all your hopes and your best efforts seem to end in disappointment and you can't get through the door you've been trying to open, all of a sudden another door will open up right in front of your face.

Even if you hadn't planned to go through that door, you can see that you're supposed to. The thing to do in that situation is to go on through the door. Don't question the purpose or the reasons at that point; just accept it. It is probably the door you should have gone through to begin with, and I believe this is one of the main ways we can experience God's leading in our lives.

Going Where You're Wanted

One of the best examples I can give of this type of situation is the story of how we ended up building our baseball stadium for the Charlotte Knights minor league baseball team down in South Carolina. In the beginning I really wanted to build our new stadium in Charlotte. I tried everything I knew to buy the land and bring the team to our home city, but we were blocked at every turn. There were roadblocks everywhere I looked, so I eventually decided that the only way I could get the team back in action was to go across the state line and build the stadium there.

The actual site is only two miles from the Charlotte city limits, eleven miles from uptown Charlotte, and just off a major interstate freeway. It is a spectacular new stadium with state-of-the-art facilities. It wasn't what I had in mind in the beginning, but it was what we could get. As it turns out, the decision to go south really helped our Charlotte fans to understand how serious we were about AAA baseball. It showed the strength of our commitment to the game, and furthermore, it helped build new bonds of friendship with the people of South Carolina that we couldn't have built any other way.

The door I *wanted* to open was here in Charlotte. I wanted to build a stadium right next to the Charlotte Coliseum. We could have used the same parking. We would have been right next to the Charlotte Airport, so all the airplanes flying over could look down and see our beautiful facility, and in my mind's eye I could already see it just that way. I thought that the synergy of having our people at the Hornets working with the management of the baseball franchise would be a big plus for us. But it wasn't to be.

For some reason, members of the old guard in our city,

along with some of the politicians, didn't like any of our plans for the baseball team, and every time I walked up to their door and tried to get in, it was locked and bolted. I simply could not get in, no matter how hard I tried.

About the time that I was becoming utterly frustrated with the way things were going, I was invited to come down to South Carolina to speak to a group of civic leaders at a breakfast for business leaders in York County. It was one of their annual events, and I went down to give a motivational speech. But obviously this was a setup.

As soon as I finished my remarks, five of the prominent leaders in the area began making speeches of their own, to me. The mayor, an officer of the chamber of commerce, a representative from the governor's office, and two other men stood up to tell me about the advantages of building in their state. Before I knew what had hit me, a door opened up right next to the one I had been trying to open.

> Before I knew what had hit me, a door opened up right next to the one I had been trying to open.

They said, "Mr. Shinn, we want you to consider putting your baseball stadium here in York County. We know you've been trying to build it in Charlotte, but we want you to come to South Carolina. We'll do everything we can to make this an easy decision for you."

Everybody wants to be wanted, and as I listened to their presentation, it crossed my mind that the leaders of Charlotte didn't really want our ballpark at all. At least they were doing everything in their power to block my efforts at every turn. I had offered to build the stadium with my own money and then to donate the property back to the city, but they wouldn't have anything to do with it.

My only stipulation had been that if I built the stadium, I would have control of the facility. I had said, "You are all businessmen, and I'm sure that if you put up your money for a beautiful new facility, you would want to make sure you could operate it the way that's best for your business interests. You don't want someone who hasn't invested their own funds telling you how to manage your business. If I put up my money and build this new stadium, I assure you it will draw fans and visitors to our city, but I will want to have control of it." They had listened, but they had refused.

I had a baseball team waiting for a home, and they had a season to play, so I finally made the only choice I could. The people in South Carolina not only agreed to my terms, but they helped me find the land and expedite the paperwork. They assigned a task force to help select the site and put in the infrastructure, and they even agreed to put in all the roads that would be needed to make access safe and convenient.

In the end, I wound up buying a lot of land adjacent to the site for future development. Today, we have about one hundred acres around the stadium, and we just completed a spectacular new practice facility for the Charlotte Hornets at the same location. We have put a lot into it, and I can assure you that no team in the NBA will have a better or more comfortable place to work out.

Where There Is No Way

When I saw that the door I wanted to go through was nailed shut, I eventually had to accept that fact. I decided that in his infinite wisdom, God knew what was best for me. A couple of times I have used this example: I wanted to take the prettiest girl to the prom, but she wouldn't go with me. When I looked around, there was another girl who was pretty cute, and she was eager to go with me. I'd be better off and have a lot more fun with the one who wanted me than I would with the one who didn't. When I had tried my original idea and it didn't work, then the smartest thing was to move on to plan B. That's what I did, and I'm convinced now that I got the best girl after all.

A couple of times already in this story I have mentioned that sportswriters seem to love to go on the attack, and they

55

really tried to drill me when I announced the plans to build our ballpark in South Carolina. "Here goes Shinn again," they said. "He's out of his mind. Nobody in his right mind would drive across the line to South Carolina to watch minor league baseball." But once again they were wrong.

The first year the Charlotte Knights played at the new stadium in South Carolina, we led the entire league in attendance. Each year thereafter we led all AA baseball teams in attendance, nationwide, and now we've moved up to AAA status, which is the next step to the big leagues. I will talk more about the Knights in a later chapter—they are one of the hottest teams in the minors today—but you would think their success would have made believers out of our detractors. Not so.

> As anyone can see, we now have one of the finest baseball parks in the country.

The sportswriters have never mentioned any of this or said, "Shinn might have been right!" They never admitted that they had guessed wrong, but I have learned to take that in stride. In fact, those kinds of things motivate me. To get people to come, I didn't just want to build a facility; I wanted to build a first-class facility. As anyone can see, we now have one of the finest baseball parks in the country. Even the major league scouts, coaches, and owners who come to our park are impressed with the space and comfort of the Knights' Castle.

It is a flexible design that will allow us to grow to major league status if that ever becomes an option. The infrastructure for a major league park is already in place, and the stadium is expandable. From the existing structure we can add upper decks, boosting seating capacity up to forty-five thousand, and all seats are first class. The fashion designer Alexander Julian, who designed the uniforms for the Charlotte Hornets, selected the colors and helped us lay out the facility. From the air, it looks absolutely beautiful—it looks a little bit like an Alexander Julian sweater!

We use the team colors in the stadium to help people find their seats—the ballpark is color coded. Most minor league parks have either concrete banks or benches to sit on, but we have armchair seats for every fan in the stadium. From the bathroom facilities to the kitchens and the parking, we did it first class all the way. Not only is it pretty, but it is highly functional. The fans, the players, the coaches, and the employees are all happy there. And it is perfectly obvious now that this was the right thing to do and the right place to do it.

But enough. I'm getting ahead of myself. The point I want to make here is really quite simple. If you have faith and if you believe in yourself, God has the power and he can provide a way where there is no way. He may fulfill your dreams beyond your wildest expectations, or he may have a completely different plan for your life. I am convinced that God is responsive to people who are willing to exercise their faith, challenge their difficult circumstances, and give it their best shot. It may not happen overnight, and it may not happen the way you expect it to, but sooner or later, the right and best thing will come along.

That's a lesson I learned at my mother's knee when we were struggling to keep food on the table, and it is a lesson that has taken me a long way in life. I sincerely recommend it to you as well.

5

Seeing the Upside of a Down Situation

WHEN I started to work as a recruiter at Evans Business College, I had the feeling that I was starting a whole new chapter in my life, and I was. The owner of the school at that time was a man named W. D. Ratchford. Dave Ratchford was the man who gave me the motivational books that started me thinking that I might have some hidden potential within me and that if I applied myself, I could accomplish more than my track record so far suggested.

When I read *Think and Grow Rich* by Napoleon Hill and *The Power of Positive Thinking* by Norman Vincent Peale, I began to understand that we all start out with the same basic opportunities. It doesn't matter whether you're rich or poor, or whether you have a great education or any other advantages. What matters most is what you do with the talents you have and how you develop yourself in order to achieve your fullest potential.

I believe you can learn important lessons from everything that happens in your life. I recognized that the principles my mother had taught me as a child were helping me, and thanks to the writings of Norman Vincent Peale and others, I basically understood that faith should be important as well. All these things helped to get me on the right track, but I still had a lot to learn about business, life, and faith.

I enjoyed my job very much, and I proved early on that I was going to be good at it. I was recruiting record numbers of students for both campuses of Evans Business College, and little by little my financial situation was beginning to improve. My personal relationship with Mr. Ratchford was very good at first. In some ways he seemed like the father I never had, but things were destined to change as I began to achieve more and more success.

Even though he was the owner of the school, Ratchford didn't actually work there in the beginning. He was involved in politics and the legal system in our area. He had a lot of supporters at that time and was elected clerk of the superior court. He was a person I really admired and looked up to. I thought the world of him as an individual, and he was also a leader in one of the most prominent Presbyterian churches in Concord. There is no question that he was a highly revered member of the community.

While I was working at the college, he left the position in the court in order to become president of the largest financial institution in the county—a savings and loan. Along the way he took me under his wing and told me many stories and shared some important principles with me that helped to develop my business career.

Learning to Focus
Once I took over the primary recruiting duties at the school, I was given the title of director of admissions, which meant

that I was in charge of all recruiting and admissions activities for all our campuses. I really loved what I was doing. I was learning to use my natural talent as a salesman, and I was helping young people who might not otherwise get an education to do so. Over the years, that has become more and more important to me.

One of our responsibilities was to help the students get jobs through the Placement Department. We worked with various people who would interview students, and there was one particular man who hired our students on a regular basis. We had an understanding, though, that he wouldn't try to hire them full time until they had completed their coursework.

On one occasion, however, he violated our agreement. His company had hired one of our brightest students on a part-time basis while she was still in school. She turned out to be such a good employee that he broke his promise and talked her into quitting school and going to work full time. Needless to say, we were all very upset. The young woman was a good student, she was good for morale, and she was one of those people you hate to lose, especially in that way. So I let this man know that I was disappointed and upset that he had broken his word to me.

> *I was learning to use my natural talent as a salesman, and I was helping young people who might not otherwise get an education to do so.*

Mr. Ratchford, who was twenty years my senior, wiser, and better educated, got together with me one day and asked me to sit down and talk things over. He said he wanted to tell me a story.

"You grew up on a farm, didn't you, George?"

I said, "Yes, sir. In Kannapolis."

"Well, George," he said, "have you ever seen a stream where the water is so clear and pretty that you can just reach down your hand and grab a drink of water that's cold and clear and delicious? Have you ever seen that?"

I said, "Why, sure I have."

"Well," he said, "what would happen to that stream if the farmer was walking his cows back to the barn, and just as they were crossing that stream, some of those cows dropped some patties in the water? What would happen then?"

"I suppose the water wouldn't be fit to drink for a while," I said.

"You're exactly right, George," he said. "Why, all of a sudden that water would be ugly and messy, and you wouldn't want to walk through it, much less drink it. Isn't that so?"

"Yes, sir," I answered. "That's true."

"But you know what?" he continued, looking me in the eye. "If you let it pass for a while, in a few days that stream will be as nice and clear as ever, and all that nasty business will pass on through, and it won't amount to much anymore."

It was certainly a novel way to get his point across, but I could see what Ratchford was trying to tell me. By raising such a ruckus with one of our most important friends and benefactors, I was making a mess of things. This man could employ a lot of our students, which was our lifeline. That homespun story helped me to see the situation with new eyes. Here I was, yelling and screaming about one student's leaving school before she graduated. But by making an issue of it, I was creating problems with someone who could do our schools a lot of good for years to come.

That was an example of the kind of advice Dave Ratchford gave me. More than once he helped me see the reality of some of the situations I would run into. For obvious reasons, I have never used that particular story in any of my speeches, but I think it makes a pretty good point.

Changing Rules and Roles

That's the way our relationship started out. As the schools started to increase in enrollment, I started working longer and harder, and I was traveling to all the various campuses on a fairly regular basis. I was making a positive contribution to the school, so eventually Ratchford let me buy in as a partner. By this time he owned schools in Durham and Greensboro, and there was a chance for us to buy another one in Fayetteville, so I spent a lot of time putting those deals together.

Before long, we bought a school in Raleigh, King's Business College, which was the oldest proprietary school in the state—founded in 1901. Later, we acquired another in Gastonia. We had all these schools, but our financial problems were just getting worse and worse, so we decided we needed to divide up and try to manage our schools separately. Mr. Ratchford would run the Gastonia-Concord school, my friend J. L. Brooks would take over the Fayetteville school, and I took the Raleigh-Durham-Greensboro schools, along with most of the debts.

> *It was clear that we were going to have to make some serious changes somewhere along the line if we expected to stay in business.*

Now, I believe in dreams, but I don't think dreams come true unless they're backed up with muscle. Although Dave Ratchford was a dreamer too, often he didn't back up his dreams with practical plans or solutions. Instead, he tried to get other people involved in his schemes and used them to make his dreams come true. I think that you have to make your own dreams come true. I could never communicate that to Ratchford.

It seemed we were always struggling with money. As soon as we got a little bit ahead, Ratchford would take the money out of the company, and we'd be back in trouble all over again. At the same time, he was hiring unworthy people and bringing in people we couldn't trust. It wasn't long before we had our backs up against the wall, financially and in every other way. This became a powerful learning experience for me—a warning about what *not* to do and how *not* to run a business.

At one time we were kiting checks, running from our creditors, robbing Peter to pay Paul, and every other cliché I can think of. It was an awful time. We managed to buy another school in Raleigh, but it was clear that we were going to have to make some serious changes somewhere along the line if we expected to keep up enrollment and stay in business.

The first thing I tried was starting an athletic program. We fielded baseball, basketball, and even football teams, and went up against college freshman teams, prep schools, junior colleges, and any other schools we could get to play us. It was a costly undertaking, but it was a good experience that helped us recruit new students. Ironically, this was my first experience managing sports teams. In a limited way, it was my first exposure to the field that would eventually become my principal occupation. (As a sidelight to that experience, a few years ago a gentleman named Giles Moss, who was running for county alderman in Concord, gave a campaign speech in which he boasted that he had played on George Shinn's first basketball team!) Well, the students in that school weren't exactly the caliber of the Charlotte Hornets, but they were a scrappy bunch of kids, and we all learned a lot from the experience.

Despite all that effort, we kept losing money, and I knew something had to happen. What I did was to start looking for someone who could help me get a better view of our situation, someone with experience in this business who had a better perspective. I started traveling, visiting other schools that were successful. At that time the undisputed leader in the proprietary-school business was a man named Jack Jones, who owned a string of schools in Florida. Jack Jones had the best schools, the best reputation, and the best caliber of graduates in the industry in those days. He was a great public speaker and a leader in the proprietary-schools association. If anybody had the edge and was on top of the business, it was Jack Jones. He was the kingpin. Nobody could match his record of success, and I knew I could learn something from his operation if he would talk with me.

The outstanding part of Jones's system was the program he had developed for recruiting Vietnam veterans who wanted to go back to school and prepare to reenter the workforce. His concept was unique and it really made his operations stand out, especially after Congress passed legislation that allowed veterans to use their GI Bill eligibility to pay for two-year programs, technical schools, and business colleges like ours. I had met Jack a time or two in the line of business, so one day I called him at his office in Florida.

"Jack," I said, "I can see all the great things you're doing with your schools, and it's obvious that you have developed some wonderful programs. The fact is, I've really been struggling up here, and I need some help with my business. Can you help me, Jack? I have heard that if a man would extend his hand to you, you'd be willing to help him out. And, Jack," I said, "I'm reaching out to you."

He didn't hesitate. "That's no problem, George," he said. "I'd be happy to give you some pointers. Come on down here to Jacksonville, and we'll take a look at what you're doing, and if I see someplace where I might be able to offer some suggestions, I'd be happy to give you a hand."

Blessings in Disguise

I was thrilled. Finally, here was somebody who knew what was going on and who was ready, willing, and able to help me. So I scheduled an appointment, booked my flight to Jacksonville, and flew down to meet him on the appointed day. I got a taxi and went over to his office and introduced myself to the secretary.

She gave me a puzzled look and said, "Are you sure Mr. Jones was expecting you today, Mr. Shinn?"

The question took me by surprise. "Yes, I'm sure he is," I said. "We made an appointment, and he offered to help me with some business matters."

She looked at the appointment book on her desk, and clearly there was nothing scheduled for that day. "I'm sorry, Mr. Shinn," she said, "But Mr. Jones is not here today. He's out of town and he won't be back until later this week. I'm afraid there's been some mistake. Maybe he forgot."

"I hope I haven't made a mistake," I said. "I just flew down here from North Carolina because I thought I had an appointment with Mr. Jones. He was going to give me some tips on running my schools." But I was wasting my breath. Somehow or other, Jack Jones hadn't written our appointment down in his book and he was out of town. So I put my tail between my legs, got a taxi back to the airport, and flew home in utter dejection.

The next day Jack called me at the office and apologized. "George, please forgive me," he said. "I absolutely forgot about our meeting, and I'm really embarrassed. I want to make it up to you. You tell me when you can come back down here, and I'll buy you a plane ticket. And this time, I promise I'll be there, and we'll see if there's not some way I can help you out." That's just what he did.

> Today I believe that embarrassing situation may have been a blessing in disguise.

Thanks to that missed appointment, Jack opened up all that much more. In fact, today I believe that that embarrassing situation may have been a blessing in disguise because Jack really took our meeting seriously and he shared some wonderful ideas with me.

We became best friends as a result of that experience. He helped me see our mistakes more objectively and showed me everything he was doing, and that turned out to be my first big financial blessing. When I got back home to North Carolina, I started applying those principles, fine-tuning them to meet our particular needs. I improved on some of Jack's recruiting methods, the types of courses we were offering, and many other things.

By this time I had three schools of my own. A short time later, J. L. Brooks's school up in Fayetteville went bankrupt, and I went up there to see if I could help him out. Enrollment in our schools was turning around and things were picking up very fast, but I didn't have the cash at that time to get the Fayetteville school up and running.

There was a lawyer in the area, however, named Charles Rose, who I thought might be able to help. He is the father of the congressman Charlie Rose. I went to see him, told him about the problem with the schools, and said I needed some help. I told Mr. Rose I needed $10,000 and that I had already been to all the banks and they wouldn't give me a loan.

There was a bank right across the street from his office, and Mr. Rose asked me if I had been there yet. I said, yes, I had. He said, "Who did you talk to?" I told him, and he said, "Well, go back over there."

So I went back. Thanks to his call and his agreement to sign a note for me, I got the $10,000 I needed. That loan was the thing that finally pulled us out of the hole and got my schools back on solid ground. As a result of that experience, Charles Rose and I became good friends. As I became successful over the next few years, he called me from time to time to come up and speak at his church or civic groups, and I never turned him down.

That was the first major turning point for me in business. I had worked hard, I got some lucky breaks along the way, and there were several generous people who had offered a helping hand. Had I failed and had the schools gone under, that might have been the end of my story. But at that critical moment, when I desperately needed a hand, a good and godly man had confidence in me and was willing to go out on a limb for me.

Turning Things Around

I ended up hiring J. L. Brooks to come to work for me, and he directed the business end of the schools for several years. J. L. and Britt Dorman were trusted allies who worked with me in the development of my network of schools, which grew to thirty over a period of time. Many of our systems were revolutionary, and I ended up founding a consulting practice that was the most influential organization of its kind in the country. It was during that time that my financial holdings began to multiply, and our system for operating proprietary schools was the dominant force in the industry.

Since that time there have been a lot of changes in all our lives. J. L. Brooks went into a business of his own for a while. He was one of the best managers I had ever met, and I knew that someday we would work together again. As it turned out, the opportunity to bring J. L. back was the invitation from the trustees of Barber-Scotia College to help reorganize their financial and administrative systems.

Barber-Scotia is a historic black college in our area, and some of our area's most distinguished citizens are alumni. The directors wanted to start a business-education program at the college, using one of my books and a leadership-development course I had written a few years earlier. I said I'd be glad to help, to contribute some money, and to help set up a leadership-development center on campus.

In fact, I said I would even teach the course for free. But, I said, I'd like to have some input into the people they picked to run the center. They agreed, so I asked them to hire J. L. Brooks, which they did, and I set up the account to pay his salary.

Today, J. L. is administrator of the leadership program at Barber-Scotia, working with Britt Dorman, who had been the president of my schools before I sold them. They are two of the best and most qualified school men I have ever met, and they are eminently qualified to help Barber-Scotia develop its programs and facilities.

The college has been through some tough times in recent years, and in mid-1994 we had to replace the president and make some major management adjustments. I knew that J. L. and Britt could help get things back in order, and I was pleased when the trustees agreed to bring them on board. But I suspected there might be some doubts or reservations.

When I spoke to the directors, I was direct. I said, "Ladies and gentlemen, I know that some of you may not think that J. L. and Britt are the right color since they're both white, but

I truly believe they're the right men to help you accomplish your goals. You won't find anybody better at running this college, putting together budgets, or keeping people productive.

"Britt Dorman knows how to get things back on a sound financial basis," I said. "He has a comprehensive knowledge of the school business, and he has worked with minorities all his adult life. If the person you choose has got to be African American, then don't pick him. But if he just has to have the right experience, principles, and beliefs, then Britt is the man you're looking for. Along with the skills and dedication of a man like J. L. Brooks, I'm confident you'll soon discover that you've got a winning combination here." The board voted on it, and they agreed unanimously to hire them.

> *It is important to identify with the people you want to help; but it's just as important that they identify with you.*

In mid-1994, while we were still trying to get all the financial systems set up, I called Rev. Jesse Jackson and asked him to come down and speak to the faculty and student body at Barber-Scotia. Part of the reason the school was having financial difficulties was that some of the key people seemed to have lost hope, and little by little that attitude spread to students and others. There seemed to be an attitude of defeatism, of lost faith, and of fear of inevitable collapse. I knew that Jesse Jackson could get the attention of the students and faculty at Barber-Scotia because he had been there. He knew only too well what hardship and struggle are all about, and I was certain he could offer some encouragement.

I know from my own experiences what it is like to grow up with poverty, with humiliation, and with a less-than-ideal education. I could offer my own encouragement to those students, and I did. But since the majority of the students and faculty at Barber-Scotia are African American, they were more likely to listen to someone like Jesse Jackson, who had

69

been there himself, than they were to listen to me. Jackson knows firsthand the problems that blacks face in our society, and he is an eloquent speaker.

Jesse knew it wasn't a good idea to give the students and faculty a handout unless they were willing to make a positive contribution to their own goals. He challenged the students to give their own money to support our efforts. He said, "You can't expect other people to put money into this institution unless you show them that you believe in it too. So I want to know: How many of you will be willing to give a hundred dollars to help support this school?" Dozens of people all over that room, from the faculty, staff, and the student body, rose to their feet to tell Jesse that they cared and wanted to do their part.

Something to Shoot For

It is important to identify with the people you want to help; but it's just as important that they identify with you. That was no doubt a critical factor in the success of my schools during the 1970s. When students found out my background and when they saw that I had been able to step out of financial hardships and build a successful career, they began to see that they could overcome their problems too.

"Here's a guy who had to have help from welfare," they said, "who finished last in his class, and now he's rich! He has a lot of influence, and he made a success of his life. Why can't I do the same thing?" That was the very point that I wanted to get across to them, and that message became a tremendous marketing tool for us as we built the business from one small school in Concord, North Carolina, to thirty schools all over the South. Little did I know when I was going through those difficult times as a child in Kannapolis that the very things that hurt me the most would someday be the things that would enable me to help others.

When I sold my schools a few years ago, I put a clause in the contract that stipulated that the new owners would keep my people on board for a certain period of time. I did that for two reasons: first, to protect the employees and give them a chance to prove themselves, and second, to ensure that the new owners would have some continuity and security in running the business. The last thing they should do would be to let the current management go and start off with no knowledge of the systems that were already in place.

As soon as that contract was up, the new owners fired my people, and today those schools are all closed. The price they paid for that decision was seeing their business go down the tubes.

After my meeting with Jack Jones, but before we really started turning things around, Dave Ratchford started asking me for financial help. He had made some bad business decisions and he was struggling financially. He needed a car, some clothes, and various other things. I ended up buying him some tailored suits, leased a new Buick Electra for him, and gave him a substantial amount of cash. But he still wanted more. He became very demanding.

When I filled my attorney in on what was happening, he chewed me out royally for what I was doing. He said, "George, have you lost your mind? You don't owe W. D. Ratchford a thing, and you're doing both yourself and him a terrible disservice trying to satisfy his demands. You have made him dependent on you, but you've got to stop being Santa Claus. You have got to break this cycle of dependency. That's my legal advice, George."

I understood what he was saying, but actually taking my lawyer's advice wasn't going to be as easy as it sounded. I knew it was going to be an exceptional challenge to turn this situation around.

6

Seeing the Light

IN reality, my lawyer was only confirming what I already knew. I decided I would go ahead and pay off the car I had been leasing for Ratchford and give it to him. I was doing very well in business and our schools were making money, so I sent him some cash. Not only were my schools doing well, but the consulting business was doing extremely well, and I felt I could give Ratchford one good send-off before I cut the strings.

But Ratchford must have sensed that I was about to cut him off, because he started yelling that I owed him money. He claimed we had made an agreement, and I was supposed to pay him 10 percent of everything I owned and earned. He couldn't produce such an agreement, of course, because it didn't exist. He said it was an oral agreement, but I told him that was ludicrous.

"I might not be the most educated person in the world," I said, "but, Dave, I'm not stupid. And no one in his right mind would ever make you a promise like that! I have always been willing to help you," I told him, "but I can't carry you forever, and I'm certainly not going to give you 10 percent of everything I earn!"

I felt genuinely sorry for him. But he said, "I gave you the methods you're using to recruit your students. You owe me for that."

"Dave, you know very well that Jack Jones was the one who gave me the methods I'm using today, and he will confirm that fact." In fact, Jones had given me the credit for formalizing his concepts and marketing them. But Ratchford wouldn't listen. He insisted that we had an oral contract when that was simply not the case. It didn't become much of an issue until one time when Ratchford decided to force a public confrontation.

I had agreed to speak one Sunday at Oakhurst Baptist Church. They ran a little ad with my picture in the newspaper, inviting people to come out and hear me speak. When I arrived at the church that morning, I went back to the pastor's study. I hadn't been there very long before one of the deacons came in and said there was some kind of disturbance in the sanctuary. The minister went out to see what was going on. He came back in a few minutes and asked the deacons and the other people in the room to step out for a moment.

He said, "Mr. Shinn, there is a Mr. Dave Ratchford sitting on the front pew, and he wants to talk to you. He said if you don't talk to him, he's going to disrupt our service."

Needless to say, I was surprised, but I went out to see Ratchford and find out what was going on. He had a yellow legal pad on which he had written out a contract in his own hand. He held it out to me and said, "You sign this, George Shinn, or I'm going to stand up and tell the whole world what kind of person you are."

I couldn't believe my ears. Naturally I refused to sign the paper, and I said, "This is ridiculous, Mr. Ratchford, and you know it. But most of all, I resent the fact that you would come here into the house of God and threaten me in front of this congregation. What kind of person are you?"

He just scowled at me, so I said, "You go ahead and do what you've got to do, Dave, but if you stand up in front of these people and say those things, it will say a lot more about you than it will about me." I turned and walked away. I went back to the study to tell the minister what was going on.

I said, "I don't think I should speak today, Reverend, because it will just cause problems and embarrassment for everyone here. If there's anyone out there who came here to hear me speak, they're not going to be very impressed if this man creates a scene in front of the whole church. So I think I had better leave."

I went ahead and spoke that morning, even though my stomach was churning.

The preacher said, "I understand, Mr. Shinn. I'll take care of it. Please wait for me."

What he did was to walk outside and speak to the police officer who was directing traffic for the church. He said, "There's a man in the front pew who is disrupting our service and making a spectacle of himself in front of the congregation. I think it would be a good idea if you escorted him out of the church." And that's what he did. The policeman went down to the front, took Ratchford by the arm, and told him that if he didn't leave quietly, he was going to be hauled off to jail for causing a public disturbance. Ratchford grumbled and tried to argue, but he finally left and the officer made sure he didn't come back.

I went ahead and spoke that morning, even though my stomach was churning. Here was a man I had always held in

75

high regard. Over the years I had looked up to Dave Ratchford almost like a father, and his behavior and his irrational demands really cut me to the quick.

Preserving Appearances

After that incident things went from bad to worse, and we ended up going through a troublesome lawsuit. It was a dreadful experience for me. How could this happen? Someone for whom I had so much admiration and respect was blaming me and accusing me of all sorts of things, and I was having to defend myself at no small expense. Then, just when it seemed it was going to drag on forever, Ratchford had a heart attack and died. It happened instantly.

I felt a sudden rush of emotion—a mixture of sorrow and relief. It was tragic that he should die like that, leaving behind a wife and two college-age daughters. But I couldn't help but be relieved that the litigation would at last end. But that's not what happened. As soon as the funeral was over, Ratchford's lawyers let it be known that they were continuing the suit on behalf of his widow, and they intended to drag me through the courts. They had no intention of giving up, since they believed there was money to be made.

My attorney went over to meet with these guys, and when he came back, he said, "George, I have worked out a settlement for this thing if you are willing to go along."

"If it involves paying them any more money," I said, "I don't want anything to do with it. If I do that, it will make it look as if I have something to hide. It will make people believe that I did something wrong. And you know that's not the case."

"Well, it does involve some money," he said, "but it's not a lot of money, and it is money to help his widow, Mrs. Ratchford." He told me the family needed $20,000. That was their only request.

I said, "Well, if it is to help her settle Ratchford's debts, I'll do it."

"And there's just one more thing, George," my lawyer said.

"It also involves helping Mrs. Ratchford get a job, even if you have to hire her yourself."

After thinking about it for a minute, I agreed. "I don't know what qualifications she has, but I'll do whatever I can to help her." As it turned out, I brought Bonnie Ratchford into my office and gave her a job working as one of our secretaries. When she came, I knew that there was a chance there might be some bitterness, and if that was the case, it was going to be difficult to work with her. So I brought her into my office, and I sat down with her and tried to clear the air.

"Bonnie," I said, "you and I never talked during all of these legal battles, but I know you loved Dave very much. I understand that, and I want you to know that I did too. And I feel it is very unfortunate that all this had to happen. I am not going to sit here and tell you I was not at fault for anything that happened. I don't want to try to paint the picture that your husband was all wrong and I was right. I'm not going to do that, in respect to Dave's memory."

She said, "I appreciate that, George."

"However," I said, "if we're going to work together, we're going to have to get along. Do you agree?"

She said she did. So I said, "Bonnie, I want you to know that I don't know everything that happened, but there is one thing I can tell you for certain. I'm sorry it happened, and I'd like to put all that stuff behind us now. And since you are working for me now, I'll do everything I can to help you."

I saw her on a daily basis over about the next four or five years, and we never had a cross word. The last I heard of her was when she announced to the staff that she was getting remarried. I never met her new husband, but I called to say that I wished them good luck and God's blessings on their new life. And I also wanted to tell her husband what a wonderful lady he was getting.

The Power of Faith

One of the basic principles of education that we employed in the school business is that you can't force people to learn.

You can force them to do certain things, and they may go through the motions for you, but it won't be authentic, and chances are it won't last. It's only wasted motion. If, on the other hand, you can somehow motivate them to *want* to learn and if somehow they decide that they want to make something out of themselves, then they become the architects of their own dreams. That's when real learning takes place.

Sometimes students say they can't afford the tuition, housing, transportation, meals, and all the other things it takes to stay in college. I am always quick to point out that they always seem to be able to afford the things they really want. If they want a fancy new outfit, they can afford it. If they want a new stereo, they can afford it. And if they want a car, you can bet they'll find some way to get it. You can always afford what you really want.

> **You can always afford what you really want.**

If you don't believe that, next time you see a group of students hanging around the local mall, look at their backsides and notice what they're wearing. You'll see designer jeans, expensive sneakers, or maybe an expensive jacket. They can't afford those either, but they want them. And if they want them, they'll find some way to pay for them.

By the same token, if they want an education, they'll find a way to pay for that too. Just think what would happen if we could somehow instill in these kids' minds the desire and the need for an education. What if we could make the process of learning so stimulating and rewarding for them that they would start wanting to learn on their own without being pushed? When they want an education, they'll get it. That's part of the philosophy we developed in our business schools.

My mother understood this principle and, intuitively I suspect, used a subtle form of motivation to help me understand the importance of faith in my life. When I was in high school, I decided I didn't want to get up on Sunday and go to church. I think I understood the importance of faith at the time, but I didn't want to go to church. Maybe it was just natural rebellion; I don't know. Mama would always remind me on Saturday night, but she wouldn't force me to go. Sometimes she would leave a note on my bed the night before, and when I came in, I would see the note: "Do you want to go to church tomorrow?" I'm sorry to say that more often than not the answer was no.

I'm sure she was disappointed with my choice. She gave me the right to make up my own mind, but she also reminded me that things wouldn't always be that way. "At your young age you don't realize just yet how important it is to have a relationship with God," she said, "but there's going to come a time in your life when you're going to need him." And to be sure I got the point she would say, "Remember, George, God has a way of looking after his regular customers."

I remembered those words and they made an impression, even if I didn't fully understand. Mother always said there would come a time when I would really need God in my life, and I would find that he would seem a little nearer if I had been walking with him faithfully. But she never pressed the point too far, which was good. If she had forced me to go to church, I think it would have made me even harder to reach. I would have resented the church, and maybe I wouldn't have opened up later on as I did.

But life has a way of teaching us lessons, if we're willing to learn. Many years later when I was talking to my financial people about acquiring an NBA franchise, they tried to talk me out of it. Everybody I knew at that time doubted that I could pull it off, and when my back was up against the wall, when I was being criticized and ridiculed by the media and the politicians in my area, the one thing that I could fall back on was my faith.

I honestly believed that the plan I was pursuing was the right one. Now, I don't claim to be perfect. I'm human and I make mistakes just like everybody else, and I want people to know that. But I believe that the biggest problem in the world today is fear, and when fear grips us and turns us away from the things that are most important—the things that can lead us to success—then fear becomes a serious liability.

There is something stronger than fear, though, and that's faith. No matter how difficult the problem may be, faith overcomes fear. I've talked to people with terminal diseases who say there's nothing the doctors can do and the only thing they have left is faith. But that should be the *good* news! If you have faith, two things can happen. Either God can cure you, which he does sometimes. Or if he doesn't do that, he can at least help you live with what you've got. Many times that's just as important as recovery. Faith is that powerful.

To some people, *faith* means some sort of blind belief or some mysterious certainty that things are going to work out a certain way. Some people get on an airplane, for example,

> "I sought the Lord, and he heard me, and delivered me from all my fears."
> Psalm 34:4

and they have faith that there's no way on earth that plane can ever fall. But I believe there's more to faith than that. Faith is not simply believing that there's opportunity and that you're going to have an abundant life and a healthy future. It goes deeper than that.

It's not possible to understand faith unless you first understand fear. In some of the talks I have given over the years, I have described the important connection between faith and fear. Fear is very real; don't let anyone convince you it's not. So many times in my life when I've faced difficult situations, people have told me, "Forget it, George. Don't worry about this problem, it's just in your mind." But that's bad advice. I have had to overcome a lot of problems over the years, and I have had to deal with a lot of serious challenges. I have had to face so many hard times there's no way anybody can convince me that fear isn't real. Fear is as real and undeniable as anything in this world.

We all have problems, and we all have fears. That's part of life. No matter how rich or how poor you may be, you're going to have problems. At this moment I may not have

80

money problems, but I have a hundred times more problems in other areas than I could have imagined a few years ago. I would never have dreamed when I first started out in business in Concord, North Carolina, that a man could be as successful as I am today and still have the problems I have. That's the way life is, and I'm learning to live with that fact.

Ten years from now I may have ten times the problems I have today, but that thought doesn't paralyze me anymore, because I know there is a way to overcome my fears, and that's through faith. Faith is the only thing stronger than fear. Psalm 34:4 is one of my favorite passages. It says, "I sought the Lord, and he heard me, and delivered me from all my fears." Faith is stronger than fear, and it is also the only way to overcome fear.

Making a Go of It

As important as these principles are to me today, it wasn't until I found myself in a terrible financial crisis that I actually made the connection between fear and faith. While I was still living up in Raleigh and before I made contact with Jack Jones, the business was really struggling to survive, and I didn't know if we could keep the doors open from one day to the next. We were so close to bankruptcy I could smell it. I had already gone a couple of months without paying my people, I couldn't pay the rent, there was no money for supplies or utilities, and we were in a desperate situation. I was still single then and didn't have any particular family responsibilities, but I was in bad shape, and I didn't know what was going to happen next.

We were getting calls from local suppliers every day telling us they were going to cut us off. They were threatening to cut off the telephones, electricity, water and sewage, and other things like that, so I went to meet with a couple of attorneys and told them all my problems. They had one recommendation: "Bankrupt this thing, George. Give it up!"

I was about thirty years old at the time. The senior partner of that law firm was a distinguished-looking older man with a striking head of white hair, and he was a formidable figure to me. When we reached the end of our discussion, he put his hand on my shoulder and said, "George, you've got a lot of charisma. You've got a lot of self-determination and guts. You know, you could be a great sales manager in any number of companies. Why don't you go out and get yourself a good job working for somebody else. You're never going to make a go of this school business."

If he had hit me in the face, he couldn't have hurt me any worse. I had some good ideas and a lot of ambition, and I knew this was the right place for me, but here was a room full of seasoned and very sophisticated attorneys telling me to bail out while there was still time. And I was paying these guys $400 to tell me I was crazy! I thought about telling them I didn't have to pay that kind of money to have somebody tell me I was nuts. I could get that kind of advice for free any day of the week! But I knew what they were saying. From their perspective what I was doing didn't make any sense.

When I left their office and walked down the hall to the elevator that afternoon, that distinguished older gentleman walked with me. He pushed the down button for me, and just as the elevator door opened, he said, "George, give it up. You don't have a prayer." Then the elevator closed on me like a jail cell. It was as if everything that I had ever dreamed of suddenly slammed shut in my face.

I felt numb. I walked to the car like a zombie. I was expressionless, tired, broke, humiliated, and desperate. I had a little Corvette at that time—which they were about ready to repossess—and I got in the car and headed toward the interstate to drive back to Raleigh. All of a sudden, the numbness went away and I started feeling scared. Deep down scared. I started shaking all over, but as I became aware of what was going on, I noticed that the sunlight was shining in through the window of the car and it was blinding me. The light was radiating through the glass like sparkles. It was because my eyes were full of tears. A rainbow of light and color was beating on my face, and suddenly I felt as if God was there with me.

It was like nothing I had ever felt before. I could sense the presence of God, and I remember that I started praying. My eyes were wide open, and I just started talking out loud. I said, "God, I don't understand why all of this is happening to me. I've tried everything I know how to do to make a go of this business, and it's not working. I'm sorry if I've made a mess of it, but I really want these schools to succeed, and I believe they can. They could help a lot of young people. . . ."

What started coming to my mind at that moment were the words my mother had spoken to me years before. *At your deepest, darkest hour, he will be near at hand. Reach out to him, George, and he'll reach out to you.* I'm not sure just what I prayed after that, but I had the sense I was communicating with God, and I made this simple promise: "Lord, I don't know what to do, but I need your help. Will you please help me? If you do, I'll give you the credit, and I won't let you down. I promise. I'll speak for you whenever I can, and I'll never forget what you have done for me."

> **What started coming to my mind at that moment were the words my mother had spoken to me years before.**

That was it. Nothing overwhelming, nothing brilliant. Just the simple prayer of a helpless man.

That was the real beginning of my relationship with God, and it's also the reason I go to church today. It's the reason I've written the books, given the speeches, contributed a portion of my income to charitable causes, and the reason we always have a prayer before Charlotte Hornets basketball games. I made a commitment to do that and I am honor bound to keep it.

But something else happened. Something quite remarkable.

When I woke up the next morning, I felt calm and refreshed, more than I had felt in years. I felt relieved. I felt as if some kind of cancer had been removed and I was healed of some deadly disease that had been choking me. I was clean and clear. I had a wonderful new feeling, and I knew that somehow, something had changed in my life. It wasn't like I had been transformed from some roughneck truck driver into an ordained minister overnight, but I felt better inside and outside, and I knew it was for a reason.

When I went back to my office, I came to work with a whole new attitude. I had been dodging my creditors for a long time, and I decided I wasn't going to do that anymore. "If any of our suppliers and creditors call," I told my secretary, "put them through."

At first she looked at me like I had flipped. But she did it, and that day I started taking calls I had refused for months. In the past I had lied to them, promising to pay bills I knew I couldn't hope to pay. Now, I decided, I was going to be honest about it. When the first call came through, I said, "Good morning. I'm glad you called this morning because I've been needing to talk to you. The fact is, I'm right at the point of bankruptcy. But don't give up on me, because I'm not giving up. I'm going to pay you. If you can just be patient a little longer and work with me, you'll get every penny I owe you."

It was incredible, and for the first time in months I could breathe freely. I started being honest with people, and as I did, the whole climate started to change. I was honest with my employees. Instead of lying to them about what was going on, I told them about the situation in detail and promised that I would pay them just as soon as I could get things squared away. I brought them in and showed them the books and everything, and I told them how I was going to try to get us back on our feet. I started asking them for their advice and help. Suddenly they were on my side.

Back to Basics

It was amazing how things began to turn around after that. One day the credit manager from a publishing company called and said that he was not going to send me any more books until I settled my outstanding debt. If I didn't have the books we needed to train our students, I couldn't do business, and that would guarantee that we would have to shut our doors. For the longest time I had begged, pleaded, even tried to run away from those kinds of problems, but this time it was different.

After I listened to his complaints, I said, "I understand exactly what you're saying, and you are absolutely right to be upset with me. I'm terribly sorry for the delays you've been getting out of us, and I promise that today I will send you what I can."

He seemed shocked but grateful that I was willing to take his call and pay my bill, so as soon as I got off the phone I sent him a check—for one dollar. Well, as you might expect, he called back as soon as he got that check and said, "What in the world is going on here, Mr. Shinn? Is this your idea of a joke? You owe me hundreds of dollars, and you sent me a check for one dollar!"

Having faith helps you think right.

"No, sir. It is no joke," I said. "I told you that I would send you what I have. That's what I have. In fact, that's all I have right now. But I am determined to pay you every penny I owe you just as soon as I can. You can count on that. The fact is, I am going through a very tough time right now, and if you cut off my supply of books, you will guarantee that we go bankrupt. But if you will stick with me just a little bit longer, until I can get a grip on these problems, then I will pay you. You have my word on that."

Can you guess what he said next? He said OK. And that was the attitude that prevailed, and that is the main reason I say so strongly today that having faith helps you think right. I hadn't been thinking right about my business in the past. Times had been so tough for so long I had begun to think like a crook. Instead of thinking and acting like an honest businessman with good business ethics, I had tried to run from my problems and dodge my creditors. I had lied about when I was going to have the money, knowing that I couldn't possibly have it that soon. I would put people off instead of dealing with them on the up-and-up. And it was killing me.

After my conversation with God that day, I decided I was going to be a good guy instead of a bad guy. Even if it meant I had to go under, I wasn't going to lie to anyone else ever again. I decided to try to do it right this time. That was another one of those pivotal points in my career.

During that time I joined the church and became more active in the life and fellowship of our congregation. I began tithing my income to the church and giving to other charitable activities, and little by little my income started going through the ceiling.

My friend Pat Clayton proposed that I consider setting up a charitable foundation to select worthy causes and distribute gifts that were appropriate to their needs. So I asked my pastor for some advice, and he introduced me to the man who would eventually become the head of the Shinn Foundation and oversee those funds.

That is the story of how my prospects changed, and it is clear to me that God was there when I needed him, just as my mother had said. If I had the faith, she told me, God has the power, and it took a terrible crisis for me to discover how right she had been.

You know the old story about God's multiplying the harvest tenfold for those who are faithful in giving to him. That first year after I got my business straightened out, I managed to clear a total of $3,000 in personal income. Things picked up over the next twelve months, and a year later I cleared $30,000. The next year, my income went to $300,000, and the next year I made $3 million. Think about it.

I eventually ended up selling my proprietary schools for $30 million. I was the sole owner at that time, but I didn't do it all by myself. There were a lot of good people working with me, and I owe them a lot of credit.

What I discovered in my car one dismal day when all hope was gone was a lesson I'll never forget. I know that God heard my cry for help, and that has made all the difference.

7
Doing Your Homework

THE chance to start out in the proprietary-school business in the early years of my career was a wonderful learning opportunity not just for the students in our schools but for me as well. It combined so many disciplines and so many different types of procedures that it gave me a chance to grow in several directions at the same time. I was responsible for day-to-day management, for marketing and merchandising the schools, for recruiting students, for financial administration, and for development of instructional programs. Each of these things stretched me and challenged me to grow, as well as helped me to gain a fundamental understanding of what it meant to be an entrepreneur.

One of the biggest advantages that proprietary schools had over the community colleges and other schools of that type, including tech schools, was that there were certain franchised programs that the schools could acquire at fairly modest cost. These were flexible, prepackaged programs that were already proven and classroom tested, and they allowed small schools to implement a top-notch instructional system that could help them build their programs and courses very quickly.

In the early years, when I was first getting involved in the schools, there was a popular course for young ladies called the Nancy Taylor Charm and Model Program. It was a good course, and some people who franchised it even called their schools the Nancy Taylor Charm and Modeling School. This type of program actually goes back to the very beginnings of the proprietary-school concept.

Years ago, when secretaries all wore white gloves to work and things were generally more formal in the business world, many young women wanted to learn poise, decorum, and business procedures. So programs like those in the Nancy Taylor Modeling Schools were essentially fashion courses, and in my early years in the business, these specialized courses were a real asset, for both the institution and its students.

They helped give young people the polish to step out into the workplace. We used to say that they helped polish the diamond and make it something that really shined. Our instructors taught them how to dress, how to put on makeup, how to walk and talk, and many other things like that. You might think of it as a somewhat more practical and career-oriented finishing school.

Mr. Cool Dresser

The people who owned the original Nancy Taylor book first turned it into a course, and then they franchised the program to business schools all over the country. Eventually, International Telephone and Telegraph Company (ITT), the communications giant, created an instructional division that ended up buying those schools and incorporating the poise and fashion program into their business and technical school curricula.

Taking some of the principles from that first course, they went on to develop another program just for men called the Mr. Executive Management Development Course. I was the first one to offer that course in North Carolina. In the early stages there were some hilarious experiences, even though I hate to admit what the real source of the humor was.

When I took the first instructor-training seminar to learn how to give the course, I had a pretty good idea of how to dress for business. In fact, up to that point I had thought of myself as Mr. Cool Dresser. I had worked part-time in a men's clothing store a few years earlier, and I knew a thing or two about fashion. Besides, I was single, and dressing well was of interest to me, so I thought I knew the ropes.

> *I was the one he picked to represent all the wrong choices.*

Maybe the instructor of that first teachers' course suspected the way I felt, because he ended up using me in one of the seminars—as a good bad example. I didn't realize what they were going to do to me until they had already started doing it. I was the one he picked to represent all the *wrong* choices. If you're tall, they said, there are certain styles of clothing you should wear, and if you're short, there are certain other styles you should wear. But there are also certain styles you should never wear, and, the teacher pointed out, I was the best example of that he had ever seen.

I was heavier at that time than I am now, and I was wearing a sport jacket instead of a suit. I was wearing loafers. My tie was a bit loud, and if there was ever an example of what not to wear in business, I was it. I don't know how he knew, but in front of the whole class the instructor said, "I bet this guy is even wearing garters." He reached down and pulled up my pant leg, and yep, I was wearing garters.

The class went wild. They absolutely loved it. I'll never forget that learning experience. In the Mr. Executive management course textbook they had pictures of Mr. Wrong Guy and Mr. Right Guy, and I was Mr. Wrong Guy at that meeting. Of course, that helped me get my act together, there's no question about it. I stopped wearing garters and sport coats, and I started wearing suits to work. I spent a little more time picking my shirts and ties to match my wardrobe.

I used to tell my students that story, and they thought it was great. I found that if you use all these things, particularly if you don't mind laughing at yourself a little bit, it really helps motivate other people and keeps them from making the same mistake you made.

Going through those various programs and courses totally changed my life. They helped me adjust and adapt the way I was operating my schools.

Keep in mind, I was going through all this when I was just twenty-three years old—and I was told that I *looked* like a teenager. I was getting an education in the real world that I could never have gotten in any school or college in the country. What I tried to do was to look and act as professional as I could, and that made a good impression in most cases. I knew for a fact that appearance and behavior would be important factors whenever I was trying to get a loan, to establish credit, or to do the other things I had to do in building my business. But it is ironic that later on, the media thought my interest in appearance was ridiculous, and they didn't spare any punches in pointing it out.

They especially made an issue of it when I landed the NBA franchise and brought the Hornets to Charlotte. Newspaper reporters, and particularly sportswriters, generally dress very casually themselves, and they ripped me because I insisted that my coaches wear suits and white shirts and that all our executives dress in business attire during the day. They wouldn't listen to my reasons. They claimed that I was a dictator, that I wouldn't let my people be themselves. But I had learned through the business schools that you only get one chance to make a first impression, and I wanted the executives and staff in my businesses, all of them, to look and act like pros.

A Positive Picture

What I was trying to do was to paint a positive picture for my team and for the community. When I went to all those meetings in New York, Los Angeles, and Phoenix, which were critical steps in winning the Hornets franchise, most people had no idea what to expect from us. They would judge us not just on our net worth, but on our appearance and behavior as well.

When they heard I was from North Carolina, they didn't know but what I might show up in a plaid shirt and a straw hat, chewing on a hayseed. For all they knew, I was going to look like Andy Griffith from Mayberry. So it was important that I paint a picture of success, professionalism, and good taste, and that's the reason we always went out of our way to look sharp. It was an expression of the philosophy I had learned while operating the business schools.

I truly believe that's one reason we were so successful in recruiting students when we were developing our business schools. We used to go to college days at some of the high schools around the state. We would see representatives from other schools and colleges and even major universities coming in dressed in golf shirts, slacks, and some of the most casual kinds of clothing you could imagine. Occasionally we saw guys wearing ponytails, earrings, and other bizarre outfits.

I remember asking one fellow, "Why do you dress like that?"

He said, "Man, you got to relate to these kids these days. You got to act like them if you want to get them."

That was apparently the way many people felt at the time, but I didn't agree. As we continued to grow in the school business, we started interviewing kids and listening to what they liked and didn't like, and I learned very quickly that they weren't looking for buddies. There were plenty of kids their own age they could hang out with. What they wanted was a school that would help them achieve their goals. They wanted a college where they could step up a notch and improve themselves. So I required my people to wear suits, white shirts, and conservative ties when we went to college days. They wore conservative haircuts and tried to look their best. "Be professional," I told them. And, yes, it was a job requirement.

As we got all our programs and plans into place, our enrollment started zooming even while enrollment at all the other schools in our region was starting to flatten out. When we asked our students why they chose our school over all the others, the reason they gave us more than any other was that our recruiters dressed and acted like successful people.

> **You gain confidence in yourself if you know you're dressed right.**

"Some of the others schools try to dress like us," they said. "That's dumb. Let us be us. And let us respect you for being you."

I don't think it's important that my coaches be the best-dressed coaches in basketball. You may know that there is a Best Dressed Coach list each year, chosen by various media people. Now, my coaches had better not be at the bottom of the list, but I certainly don't expect them to be at the top either. They don't have to wear suits all the time. That's not even the point. I just want them to look good, and to project an image that says that ours is a professional organization in a professional city with professional supporters and fans.

I'm a firm believer that if you look good, you're going to act good. And you gain confidence in yourself if you know you're dressed right. There's a time for a suit, and there's a time for a sport coat; but there's also a time for a golf shirt and shorts. There are times for all these things, and I think it's important that you know which is which.

The Vietnam Boom

While the world was changing faster than anyone could imagine, we suddenly found ourselves in the post-Vietnam era. Military veterans were enrolling in our programs in record numbers. Seemingly overnight we shot to the top in enrollment and earnings. That was an incredible growth period for the schools.

The motivation we offered to get the Vietnam vets into school was the inducement from the government, in the form of the GI Bill, and the checks they were able to get for their educational expenses. The government gave them a certain amount of money, but some of these young men just wanted to be students. Many had gone off to war straight out of high school, and they didn't have a chance to go to college or get any kind of professional training. Our schools offered a good, practical business education that would help them get jobs, and it also provided a reasonably low-stress learning environment.

Beyond the obvious advantages for us, it was also a good thing for the country at that time. Time and time again we have seen that these programs helped the young men who served in Vietnam (as well as other places) to get their careers going and to get back into the workforce. The business school environment was suited to the real world they would be going into, and the training they received allowed them to begin this new stage of their lives with confidence.

Nevertheless, after a brief boom period, which peaked sometime in the mid-1970s, the phenomenon passed and the large enrollments began slipping away. I could see that it was just a matter of time until the VA benefits would be completely gone and there wouldn't be any more veterans coming along. What I did then was to begin to look for new ways to use the programs and systems we had developed. I began thinking, *Where will the majority of our students come from during the next ten to twenty years?*

To help me find the answer to that question, I decided I needed to spend some time with the director of instructional programs at ITT. At that time the ITT schools still administered the courses we were using, and they held the rights to the textbooks and curriculum. First of all, I called the director and asked, "Do you still stock the books that I have been using in my schools?" He said, yes, they did. So I asked, "Have they been revised yet?" No, he said, and they had no plans to revise them.

"Well," I said, "if that's the case, I won't be ordering any more books from you anytime soon. I'm sure you realize," I said, "that all these books are outdated. The pictures are old and look ridiculous, and some of the students in our program feel that your course materials are not relevant anymore. But I'm curious, why won't you spend the money to update them and keep them in the marketplace?"

To make a long story short, he didn't really have a very good answer, so I asked if he would be willing to sell the rights to me. He thought about that for a while, and then said he would. So I flew up to their corporate headquarters and met with them about acquiring rights to the course materials. We had a number of conversations and negotiated back and forth, and once we settled terms and conditions, I bought all of their remaining inventory along with the rights to the course materials.

I decided to redesign those courses and rewrite them, combining the separate courses for men and women into one course and putting them into a loose-leaf binder. Photographs, artwork, questions in the text, and all the other materials were geared to our type of students. We also added a self-esteem component that helped the students realize *I am somebody.* Our students needed that message, especially during those years. We were in the business of motivating our students. We wanted them to believe that they were somebody, and we wanted them to act like they believed it.

In addition to the motivational materials, we put in a section on the "dress for success" theme that was becoming popular at that time, plus a major component on the importance of salesmanship and the power of speech. Ours was a unique approach. The decision to include a section on public speaking was drawn from my own background and my fear of reading in front of the class. That became one of the best parts of our program.

The approach we designed was practical, systematic, and nonthreatening. In the first speech class, each student had to stand up and tell his or her name. That's all. Anybody could do that. Even when I was terrified to read out loud, I could have done that. And even when I stammered, I could at least get my name out. Then the next day they had to give their name, the high school they attended, and their address. And that was it.

We gradually worked them up step-by-step until they could speak freely in front of people. The first prepared speech required them to give a thirty-second talk called "The Funniest Thing That Ever Happened to Me." Most people can tell those kinds of stories, and most people already have a couple of things to base their talk on. They don't have to do a lot of homework on a subject like that. We said, "Tell it to the class like you would tell it to your buddy. You've told it before, so you can tell it again."

> *In the first speech class, each student had to stand up and tell his or her name.*

By the end of the speech class, they were not only able to give a fifteen-minute talk to a room full of strangers but most were also comfortable talking to people one-on-one, as they would need to do in making a sales presentation or applying for a job. We went through very similar procedures with resumé writing and many other kinds of practical things that would help them get a good job.

Understanding the Market
We developed these and other programs for all thirty schools and tied the whole program in to retention, showing instructors and administrators how to retain their students for the length of

the course. All colleges and universities—as well as proprietary schools—lose the largest percentage of students after
the first semester. Since recruiting and developing a student
body from scratch each year is so costly and counterproduc-
tive, we designed our curriculum to overcome that problem.

Research told us that if the business colleges could keep
their students past the freshmen year, the majority of those
enrolled would go on to finish the course. The trick was to
keep them the first year. We worked hard on that challenge,
and as a result our retention rate went up dramatically. Once
we accomplished that goal, I knew we had something we
could sell to the industry. So I went back to McGraw-Hill,
who had first published my textbook, and asked them about
publishing a new edition for me.

I had it in a loose-leaf binder already, and it was ready to
go. All they had to do was to publish it in book form. Unfortunately, they wouldn't do it. I was disappointed. We had
bought so many books from McGraw-Hill, and I told them I
was going to buy the new ones as well for all my schools. I
said I would even help them market the course to other
schools, but they didn't want to do it.

I was so sold on the idea that I was not about to give up on
it. All those lessons I had learned as a child about faith and
about God's having the power came back to me. I realized
that the obvious solution was to publish the book myself. So
I formed a little publishing venture called Key Publishing
Company, and our main product was the textbook for our
business school curriculum.

Once we were up and running, I went to the annual convention of the Association of Independent Colleges and
Schools (AICS) and put the book on display. During the annual meeting of the AICS, literally hundreds of schools come
to find out what new systems and materials are available in
the marketplace. Thousands of college presidents and owners attend the meetings, and they come together from all
over the country. Obviously, this was the best possible place
to be seen.

We set up our booth, and that was the first time our new textbook for leadership development was ever exhibited. The booth was no bigger than a cabinet, and Britt Dorman, who was one of my associates at that time, stood there talking to people and showing the book. From the beginning, the other schools were very interested in our book. All the traffic on the convention floor seemed to converge on us. It became clear right away that we had a winner on our hands.

In the Driver's Seat

Well, it just so happens that the mighty McGraw-Hill, Inc., had their booth right behind ours, and they could see that all the action was on our side of the aisle. They had a huge display, ten times the size of ours, with at least twenty-five reps on the floor and a huge inventory of books. But we had three times the number of people coming to our booth.

Nobody missed the irony of the moment. They had just turned us down on publishing our book, so I published it myself. Their book was getting modest attention, but ours was the hit of the show. And that wasn't the end of it.

As a result of that show, the folks at McGraw-Hill called me to see if they could take another look at the project. "You know, we were really impressed that so many people seemed to be interested in your book," they said.

"Of course you were," I said, "but I told you that it was going to happen that way. There's a need in our industry for practical materials that are current and relevant to the needs of the marketplace."

They said, "What do you think, George, would you like us to publish that book?"

So I said, "It's a little late, don't you think? I've already published it, and orders are coming in like hotcakes."

"Well, then," they said, "how about if we help you market the book? We can plug it into our system, and it would be a natural for us."

Obviously, I was open to making an agreement that would be good for business, and I realized only too well that

McGraw-Hill could reach thousands more people than we could with our smaller base of operations. But their having turned me down gave me such a wonderful chance to put the pressure on!

I mean, I was in the driver's seat, negotiating with a major publisher on a product they obviously wanted, and I had a better-than-average chance of getting the kind of deal I wanted. It was a confirmation that we had produced an excellent product that would give our students and customers what they wanted.

Over the next few weeks we worked out a deal where I would get royalties at about triple the standard rate. For years that book has continued to sell extremely well, and it remains one of the top fifty books for McGraw-Hill. From day one, which was more than ten years ago, we have earned in the neighborhood of $100,000 per year from that one project.

My book on leadership development has been updated and revised a time or two, and it continues to have strong sales in the business schools. In fact, that was how I got involved with Barber-Scotia College in the first place. The president of the college was interested in using the book to teach business skills, self-esteem, public speaking, and things like that to his students. He asked me about using the course and said he wanted to develop a Leadership Center on the campus. He also wanted me to donate the first hundred thousand dollars to get it started, and since I was genuinely interested in his plan, I agreed to do it.

In the process of working out the details, I ended up being named chairman of the board, and that's where we are today. Our concerns have grown beyond the leadership program; we are also trying to reorganize some of the antiquated systems that had been in place there. We are trying to get the college on a solid foundation, both financially and institutionally. Among other things, we have plans to raise money for the college continuity fund. We raised our first million during the summer of 1994 in a matter of only a few months, and we believe that other large donations will be forthcoming.

It all goes to show that if you don't give up, your dreams are within your grasp. If you believe in your objectives, if you believe in what you're doing, and if you are convinced that what you're doing will benefit other people, then my advice is to go for it. Don't give up; just keep going, and sooner or later, you'll find a way where there were only obstacles before. It happens that way too often to be mere coincidence. It has always happened that way for me.

You don't have to bang on the same door over and over. When McGraw-Hill turned me down, I went on to the next option. I was turned down, but I didn't stop. I just went to a different door and kept on pursuing the plan that seemed appropriate until I finally got there.

I wanted to do it right, so I had hired professionals to rewrite the instructional materials. We had a nutritionist go over the parts that dealt with health and diet; a medical doctor went through the sections dealing with fitness and wellness. I hired people to edit and rewrite the narrative sections and the questions to be sure that they were timely and relevant to the interests of our students. And then I had to pay to have it published.

We used professional models for the cover photographs, and by doing all those things we eventually had a lot of money tied up in it. But it was a good product, and it was the right product for the market. Eventually McGraw-Hill wrote me a check to pay for all my development costs, plus they agreed to pay me top royalties on the product as it was being sold. The success of that project was not based on any kind of luck. It was no accident. It was based on my conviction that it was the right thing to do at the time.

8
Branching Out

I WAS doing very well in the school business, and my consulting operation took off like a rocket. In the mid-1970s we were
working with schools and recruiting programs all over the
country, and our income and investment position was very
strong. At that time Charles Ricks, the same man who would
later try to talk me out of getting too deep into the basketball
thing, came to me and said, "George, you need to diversify your
interests." So we began looking around to see what would be
the most logical fit for my situation. Because of my love for cars
and my marketing skills, we decided that the automobile business would be the most compatible with what I was doing.

When the economy is good, cars generally sell very well. If you look back at the history of General Motors, Ford, Chrysler, or any of the other major manufacturers, you will find that when the economy is doing well, car and truck sales are booming. But when the economy gets soft, people don't buy cars. If you're in the car business during a prolonged downturn in the economy, you may have to weather some tough financial times while sales are off. So you can't always count on a strong marketplace.

That's where marketing savvy becomes so important. If your business strategy is simply to sit around and cream the market when business is upbeat and the economy is soaring, you're going to find yourself in deep water when the cycle starts heading off in the other direction. You need a solid financial position and a flexible marketing program, and those were my strengths in the school business.

> *I hadn't driven it more than a month before all sorts of little problems started popping up.*

Rick Hendrick, whom I mentioned in the opening chapter, was at that time—even as a young man—one of the top car salesmen in our area. Whenever my executives and I needed to buy a car, we called Rick. He was someone we could trust, and he had a lot of charm and polish. And when we bought a car from Rick, we knew we were getting the best deal we could get. We knew Rick was going to make a little money on it, but we also knew that he wasn't ripping us off.

When we went to Rick to get a car, we bought it without haggling over the price because we knew he was giving us his best price. As a result, Rick and I developed a good working relationship long before I got serious about acquiring a dealership of my own. Here's one incident that illustrates how compatible the relationship was: One time I bought a Jaguar XKE from Rick, and I hadn't driven it more than a month before all sorts of little problems started popping up. It was a pretty little car, but it was constantly breaking down on me.

Whenever I brought it in for service, the mechanics would eventually get me back on the road all right, but within a week I would be right back again with some new problem. It was getting to be a real headache, and I let my feelings be known more than once. On one particular occasion I had driven from my home in Raleigh up to Durham, North Carolina, on business, and when I came out of my meeting, the car wouldn't start. I was beside myself with frustration. I needed to get back to Raleigh, and my whole day was going to be ruined trying to get somebody to service that car.

I called Rick Hendrick at the dealership and told him I was going to leave that car on the side of the road and if he wanted it back, he could send a wrecker to pick it up. Needless to say, they came and got it. When I got back to Raleigh, I went over to see Rick and told him I was sick and tired of playing games. I wanted my money back, I said, and if he gave me any trouble, I was going to call my lawyer and we would take him to the cleaners. It was just a nice calm discussion between two reasonable men!

If I expected a fight out of Rick, I was sadly mistaken. He was very apologetic and considerate, and he assured me he would be more than happy to give my money back. In the process of settling me down, he was so smooth that not only did I not sue him but I left his parking lot in a brand-new Mercedes-Benz. When I realized what this guy had done to me, I said, "That Rick Hendrick is smooth as silk. If I ever go into the car business, I'm going into it with him!"

Combining Our Strengths

You can't just buy an automobile franchise any old time you feel like it. It's a complicated process, and you need to be connected somewhere, so I decided that Rick would be my connection. The situation was ideal for both of us. I was eager to get into a business in which I didn't have any connections, and Rick didn't have any money. So we combined our efforts and put together a franchise proposal through General Motors. We ended up buying a Chevrolet dealership in Bennettsville, South Carolina. That first dealership was a good opportunity, and we began to learn the ropes and find out how we could work together.

Our original plan was for Rick to manage the day-to-day operations and for me to be the equity partner. However, General Motors required that the on-site dealer, the person who was going to actually operate the franchise, have at least a 25 percent interest in the business. Rick didn't have 25 percent at that time, so I loaned him the money, and that's how we first became partners.

Sometime later a dealership in Charlotte became available, so we made an offer and acquired City Chevrolet. Over the next few years we continued to expand in several directions. Rick was a natural. He was a great salesman, and he did a great job of managing the dealerships and building a loyal clientele. Along the way we added several other dealerships, including BMW, Honda, Toyota, and even Kenworth trucks.

Our business grew in every category, and our volume statistics, based on per capita sales and market saturation, were way ahead of everybody else. When Honda first came into the region, Rick could see that this was going to be the beginning of a new wave of small-sized import cars, and he jumped on it. He pursued dealerships in Columbia and Charleston, South Carolina, and in other places in our general area of interest.

We were partners on a 75/25 basis at the start, but as the dealerships boomed we eventually shifted the financial relationship and became equal partners. Along the way Rick decided he wanted to have his own store and his own identity, and he offered to buy out my interest in some of the dealerships. He was especially interested in acquiring City Chevrolet in Charlotte. When he came to me and asked if I would consider selling my stock, I said, "Rick, if that's what you want, that's fine with me. Just tell me what you think the price should be and how you want to pay me." And that's what we did.

We had a great relationship, and the dealerships were a

good opportunity for both of us to expand our horizons. I had already made a lot of money in business, and I felt that I owed it to Rick to help him grow on his own.

Somewhere along the line Rick got interested in the racing business. His first venture in that arena turned out to be racing boats. He put together a top-notch team, hired a great driver who was one of the best in the business, and before long was setting world records practically every time they went out.

But something happened. There was a freak accident during one of the major races, and Rick's driver was killed. He lost control of his boat, and it slammed into the bank and killed the guy instantly. As you can imagine, that was really a devastating experience for Rick. It wasn't long before he decided to get out of the boat-racing business. He had set up a great shop, however, and his crew was building some really fine high-performance engines, so eventually Rick decided to transition into automobile racing. That was something he had always loved. It's big throughout the South and growing in the rest of the country. He put together a team to race on the NASCAR circuit, and he is still doing very well there today.

> It became apparent before long that my interest in cars was diminishing.

We continued to expand our operations. Rick went in his own direction, doing his usual excellent job. I maintained some of the key dealerships, but it became apparent before long that my interest in cars was diminishing while Rick's was only getting bigger. Over a period of time I eventually opted out of all the dealerships and sold my interests to Rick.

During all this time I was getting more and more interested in the possibility of acquiring a sports franchise of some kind. My first goal, as I said earlier, was Major League Baseball. I suspect now that what attracted me to sports was not just the glamour and excitement associated with professional athletics but also the motivational aspects. I mean, sports *is* motivation. It is a business that succeeds or fails based on attitudes and emotions, and that was an area that appealed to me. Professional sports seemed to combine all the things I enjoyed most.

I had seen teams over the years that went to the top in their league because they demonstrated the right attitudes. I had also seen some that suffered terrible disappointments and losses because they lacked the mental toughness to win. I especially noticed those teams that had top athletes and a winning tradition but could never quite put it together when it really counted.

Some of the league's more volatile owners and managers make headlines because of the way they relate to their coaches, players, and fans. Think of people like Billy Martin, the fiery off-and-on manager of the New York Yankees, and the lightning-rod owner, George Steinbrenner. Can you imagine a more explosive combination? On some clubs, management seems to believe the way to motivate players is through fear, threats, or intimidation instead of through patient guidance, personal concern, and genuine empathy. In some operations there seems to be little or no communication taking place.

These things all came to my mind when I thought about the prospect of running a professional sports franchise. I like working with people and I know how to communicate, so I began to think that sports was something I could do well in. Not only do I love to watch sports events, I understand how to encourage and motivate people, and I have supervised some outstanding sales forces over the years. I came to believe that all these things would carry over to pro sports, and I felt it would be a natural for me.

As a youngster, I was a big Brooklyn Dodgers fan. My hero in those days was the outstanding center fielder Duke Snider. On my fiftieth birthday I got a nice little autograph from my hero. I keep it in a place of honor and it remains one of my most cherished possessions. Dodgers Manager Tommy Lasorda once said, "Cut my veins and I bleed blue, Dodgers blue." I sort of felt that way as well. I continued to follow the Dodgers after their move to Los Angeles, and I still follow them fairly regularly. Seeing how the Dodgers organization is run had a lot of influence on the way I operate today.

I guess the thing that, more than anything else, made me decide to sell my schools and auto dealerships was an article I ran across in one of the major sports magazines. It was a listing of the all the top sports franchises in the country in several sports. Based on all the key factors by which you could judge a team—championships, win-loss record, profits, player personnel, media exposure, and everything else you can think of—the writers set out to assess the best of the best, and at the very top of the list was the Los Angeles Dodgers.

I thought that was fascinating. For one thing, the Dodgers were always my special team. But there was something else that caught my eye. In each listing, along with the name of the team, their rank, and some of their notable highlights, was the name of the owner and the owner's primary business.

If George Steinbrenner had stuck to shipbuilding, he might have had fewer tensions in his life, but that is not his nature.

For every team on the list, except the Dodgers, the primary business of the owner was something other than sports. Some were in manufacturing, some were in investments or banking, and others were in real estate or insurance. But next to the name of Peter O'Malley, owner of the Dodgers, it said that his primary business, actually his only business, was the Los Angeles Dodgers. That said a lot to me.

Opportunity. That was the key word. And thinking about that helped to motivate me to sell all my other businesses over the next few years and to concentrate on sports as my primary occupation. We all have to make decisions about what we want to do with our lives. Sometimes the best decision is to trust the people we hire to do what they do best; but sometimes the best decision is to jump right in and do it yourself.

If George Steinbrenner had stuck to shipbuilding, which was his primary business, he might have had fewer tensions in his life. Or if he had just left the day-to-day management of the Yankees to his coaches and staff, things might have run more smoothly. But that is not his nature, and there is no doubt that his ongoing involvement in management makes the game more exciting for the fans. I have spent time with George in Tampa and wrote to him on one occasion that I thought the game of baseball would be less colorful without him.

But as I began to assess my own prospects as an owner, Peter O'Malley and the Dodgers were still my inspiration. Not just because they have won more games, pennants, and titles than the other teams, but because they have a team spirit that is infectious.

Another thing that increased my interest in acquiring a professional team came about as a result of my relationship with McGraw-Hill. One day a friend at the publishing house told me that Rick Honeycutt, the left-hander from the Texas Rangers who went on to become a hot pitcher for the Dodgers, was an old friend and former student of his. I had followed Honeycutt's career for years, and when I told my friend I was a longtime Dodgers fan, he arranged for me to meet Honeycutt in Atlanta when the Dodgers were in town.

I still have the pictures of Rick with my oldest son, Chris. He lifted Chris over the infield fence and took him down to the dugout to meet some of the other players. We also got some autographed pictures and other memorabilia that we still cherish to this day. Over the next few years I developed a closer relationship with Rick and found him to be a really nice guy with a sweet wife and a great family. As you can imagine, that experience just accelerated my interest in pursuing a team for Charlotte.

A Little TLC

I'm always asking people about what motivates them and why they chose one business over another. I remember asking Rick about the owners of the teams he had played for. Did he know them personally? And how were the owners of the various clubs he had played for different from one another?

"Oh, man, that's easy," he said. "First of all, on the first two or three clubs I played for, I never met any of the owners. But that changed when I was traded to the Dodgers.

"I'll never forget my first game there," Rick said. "It was my very first home game at Dodgers Stadium, and when I went through the security gate, everybody there spoke to me by name and welcomed me to the ball club. I'm talking about the security people! Everybody seemed to know me and to care that I had come to play for the Dodgers.

"But there's one thing you have to understand," he continued. "Peter O'Malley doesn't just own the *Dodgers*, he owns the stadium, too. Therefore, the security people work for him, not for the city or anybody else. O'Malley believes in creating a good work environment for his people, and he expects people in the park to be courteous and to get to know the players.

> *Treating people with kindness and courtesy goes a long way.*

"When the guard said, 'Glad to have you here, Mr. Honeycutt,'" Rick told me, "I was overwhelmed. But the best was yet to come. Before the game that night, our manager, Tommy Lasorda, came up to me and said, 'Mr. O'Malley wants to meet you,' so I went up to the owner's box to speak to him.

"I had never met any of the owners of the clubs I'd played for, George," Rick said. "But on my very first day as a Dodger, I was ushered up to Mr. O'Malley's box, and not only was I able to meet the owner of the team, shake his hand, and have him welcome me to the team, but he asked if there was anything he could do to help me get settled in. And while I was there he also introduced me to Cary Grant!"

I understood what Rick was saying. The personal touch makes all the difference. The reason the Dodgers are successful is not just because they field some of the top talent in the game but because of the way they operate, on and off the field. Treating people with kindness and courtesy—a little TLC, or tender loving care—goes a long way. And hearing that story from Rick Honeycutt made a big impression on me.

When we were negotiating our contract to lease the Charlotte Coliseum from the city of Charlotte, I told them I wanted to have some authority over the ticket takers, parking-lot attendants, and ushers, because those were the people who were going to be looking after my customers. If you want to have a team where the personal touch is visible, then it's important that everyone be treated with courtesy and respect. Personal service is not just limited to your biggest customers or your most important fans; it's the way things are done from the top to the bottom of the organization. Everybody deserves that kind of attention.

I sometimes use the example of a cup of coffee. If you take a coffee bean that was grown in the most fertile field in the richest corner of Colombia, where it was cultivated in the perfect climate with perfect care so that it becomes the best coffee bean in the entire world, and you take that perfect coffee bean and grind it in the most expensive stainless-steel grinder in the world and brew it in the best coffee percolator you can find with the purest spring water in the world, and then you pour that coffee into the finest china cup money can buy and serve it on an elegant table with the finest linen tablecloth in the nicest and most expensive restaurant in the world, and the waiter serves it without a smile, then you have an average cup of coffee.

But if you take another coffee bean that was grown right here in Charlotte, on ground that was not so fertile, and when it is dried, you grind it up in a cheap old aluminum grinder, put it in your Mr. Coffee plastic coffeemaker with water straight from the tap, and you pour it in a plastic cup and hand it to somebody seated at a Formica counter, but you deliver it with a smile, then you have the perfect cup of coffee. That's the attitude I'm talking about.

I don't care if you are selling basketball tickets, shoes, or water pumps, the attitude is the same, and the right attitude can make all the difference. Of course, you have to have a product that people want, but the thing that gives any product its value and appeal is the quality of the sales and service that come with it. Everybody likes to be treated with respect and courtesy; and what's more, everybody deserves it.

That was Rick Hendrick's secret when he talked me into trading my Jaguar for a new Mercedes-Benz. Personal service, consideration, and a willingness to help the customer solve his problem in a way that keeps him happy make all the difference. When you treat customers and fans with that kind of respect, you'll find that you can keep their business for the long haul.

My transition into the National Basketball Association didn't happen overnight, and it didn't happen by accident. It was the result of a gradual process of growth and development, an examination of my interests and talents, and a detailed study of all the factors that would help us build a top-notch sports franchise in Charlotte. From the first, the road has been long and demanding, and there were no shortcuts. I had to take every step, learning a lot about myself, my options, my abilities, my strengths and weaknesses. And it meant doing a ton of homework. But I am convinced this is where I was meant to be. It has been worth it, and I wouldn't have done it any other way.

9

Life Changes

THE first year the Hornets played in Charlotte was incredible. Opening night was November 4, 1988. We promoted it as a black-tie event, as a very special celebration, and at least 20 percent of the fans came in formal attire. Spencer Stolpen and I, and the entire staff, wore tuxedos, and so did our suppliers, the media, and most of our supporters. The crowd was into the game from the start, and even though we lost by forty points, at the end of the game they gave us a standing ovation. If you can imagine the emotion of seeing twenty-three thousand fans saying thank you from the bottom of their hearts, then you'll have some idea of how I felt. It was our first regular-season NBA game, and the excitement and appreciation of everyone in that arena was undeniable. It was one of the most enjoyable experiences I have ever had.

On December 23 we played the Chicago Bulls at home. It was Michael Jordan's first game in North Carolina since he had played here in college, and the fans knew that when he was hot, Air Jordan could beat anybody in the league. The game was a sellout, and the first game of our current sellout streak. It was an exciting game right down to the wire, and when the final buzzer sounded, the Hornets had won it by two points.

There was pandemonium in Charlotte that night. Suddenly, our fans knew we could play with the best—the Hornets were a force to be reckoned with. We have sold out every game since that time in the 1988–89 season, and there is no doubt that this was a key turning point for us. We had concentrated so much on keeping the fans happy—through high-quality entertainment, courtesy, and personal attention—throughout that first year that the Bulls victory was like a reward for all of us—fans and players alike.

> *Eight years later, the honeymoon still hasn't ended.*

Because of all the criticism that had been dumped on us in the press by writers and reporters who always seemed to be looking for negative things to write about, we often felt as if we were digging ourselves out of the cellar. Even after we started winning, the critics kept saying, "Well, they were lucky this year. Next year they're going to lose their shirts." There are some people who will just never believe. But you *gotta* believe!

The fans were faithful, and they showed that they believed in us by coming to the games and supporting their team. We've had about 99 percent season-ticket renewals every year, and we sell more season tickets than any other team in the league—more than twenty-one thousand faithful supporters. We also have over five thousand people who pay

$100 apiece to be on a waiting list called the "Hornet Hopefuls." These people aren't buying the negative press. They understand what we are trying to do.

Everybody told us that the first season would be our honeymoon year and things would change after that. But eight years later, the honeymoon still hasn't ended, and we're loving every minute of it. The measure I use to determine how well we are doing is not the criticism or skepticism of the media, but the support of our loyal customers and fans, and they continue to come out to see us play. I can't say that the barbs never sting, but I don't worry about what the reporters say, and I don't think many of our fans do either. They love their team the way I love it. They support it. They come out and cheer for us, win or lose. And I think they know I'm doing everything I can to give them a winning team.

There is a distinctive spirit among Carolinians. We take a real personal pride in our part of the country, and from the very beginning I have been trying to encourage that feeling and to stand by the people of the Carolinas. The fans know that. They have shown that they like what the Hornets are doing, and they have stuck with us through thick and thin. And they have stuck with me too.

A Time of Transition

At a time none of us will ever forget, I really needed all the support I could get. Just as I was starting to settle into a new occupation, thinking maybe I had arrived, life took a sudden, unexpected turn. It was election day, November 8, 1988, and the Hornets had a big game that night. We were playing the Los Angeles Clippers in Charlotte, and we knew we had a chance for our first win. The management executives from the area radio stations were having their quarterly meeting that afternoon, and I had been asked to come and speak about the Hornets and to give my opinion on the name change that was being proposed for the new Charlotte Coliseum.

A group of people in the travel and tourism business, and

some others who were interested in marketing our region around the country, had suggested that the name of the coliseum be changed to The Crown. The city of Charlotte is named for Princess Charlotte Sophia of Mecklenburg-Strelitz, who was the wife of King George III of England. Obviously there is a lot of history associated with that name, so these people thought the association with the queen's crown would be a marketing attraction. It was distinctive.

But since I had a vested interest in the coliseum and any name that was chosen for it, these executives invited me to speak and tell them my opinion, so I told them I was against it. My reason was simple: "I want people to identify the Hornets with the city of Charlotte," I said, "and I believe that will be much easier if we call the arena the Charlotte Coliseum."

I had researched many other teams, and I had examined all the possible names for our team long before we chose our current name. As most people know, there is a lot of history in our part of the country. The Mecklenburg Declaration of Independence was signed here in 1775, a year before the Philadelphia declaration, and the British invaded the area during the Revolutionary War. The redcoats met with such bitter resistance when they occupied our city in 1780 that the British general Cornwallis called Charlotte a "hornets' nest." That's why the city fathers put a hornet on the official city seal, and that's why we chose the Hornets as our team name. There's a lot of pride in that name around here.

If you look at teams that have generic names, using just their state or region, you will find that those teams don't win very many titles. The California Angels, for example, never generate much attendance because their fans have no clear sense of identity or relationship to the team. The state of California is too big an area to hang your team's identity on. In my opinion, the people who chose the name would have been better off had they identified with one city or metropolitan region and built on that name and history. Otherwise, the name has no appeal to any single group of fans.

When you go to NBA games in some cities, the name on the front of the jerseys is the team name. In Chicago, for example, it says *Bulls* on their jerseys, not *Chicago*. I've made it clear that my objective is to promote my city. No matter where we go around the country, whether we're playing the Knicks, the Bulls, the Warriors, the Spurs, or the Lakers, when the fans see our players, they see Hornets all right—they're the monsters on the court jamming the ball down the other team's throat! But their jerseys say *Charlotte*.

I told the writers and media people at that meeting that I understood the thinking behind the proposed name change, and I could see what they wanted to do. The main reason they brought up the idea of changing the name of the coliseum was because our old arena had been called the Charlotte Coliseum. People had begun to refer to it as "the old coliseum" and the new one as "the new coliseum."

"I think it's fine for this community to identify with the term *Crown*," I said. "Everybody who lives around here knows what that means. But how about somebody from Texas or New York or California? Will they know that The Crown is in Charlotte?" I paused, then asked, "Does anybody here know where Reunion Arena is located?" I looked around the room and no hands went up. I said, "My question has been answered. Reunion Arena is in Dallas. Everybody may know that Madison Square Garden is in New York City, but we're a new franchise, and not everybody is going to know where the Charlotte Hornets play ball unless we make Charlotte an important part of our identity, in the name of our coliseum."

> *"Does anybody here know where Reunion Arena is located?"*

There was one particular sportswriter who wouldn't let it die, and to this day he still writes about the name of the arena from time to time, saying we should have changed it. But I believed so much in promoting our city that I couldn't see giving all that away. If we were only changing the name for our own egos, to have a building named something that we

117

thought was cute or that tied in with some little-known fact of history, then it wasn't enough. It doesn't identify our area to the rest of the nation. My whole thrust was to promote and build my city, knowing that if I helped build the city, I was also building the team. Since that time the old arena has been refurbished and renamed Independence Arena, so the problem was ultimately solved.

A Matter of Life and Death

Sometime during my talk, something happened to me, and I suffered a stroke. I didn't fall down or show any symptoms at first. I never lost consciousness. The only indication I had that something was wrong was that my left arm jerked uncontrollably four or five times. It was the sort of sensation you may feel in bed sometimes when your arm or leg is cramped and you feel a jerking sensation. One person who was there told me later that at one point I appeared to be slightly dazed, but no one realized what had actually happened to me until later that afternoon.

I left the meeting after I finished speaking, got into my car, and drove back to my office. Later, my doctors told me they didn't know how I managed to drive all that way in my condition, but I did. I remember driving up to the parking deck at First Union Tower and pulling into my regular spot.

As soon as I turned off the engine, I noticed that I was covered with sweat. That puzzled me. It wasn't especially hot in the car, but I was burning up. I wondered if something might be wrong with me. Maybe I was just hungry, I thought. Maybe my system was out of balance. So I lay down across the car seat for a few minutes to regain my strength.

I remembered that I had a lunch appointment with a business associate, Mr. S. C. Hondros, and one of his colleagues that day, so after I had rested for three or four minutes, I wiped the sweat off my forehead and went up to the office. When I walked in, I noticed that the people I was supposed to meet for lunch were already there. When I get to work, I always stop and speak to people, shake hands with my associates and ask how they're doing. Spencer Stolpen, who is the president of the Hornets, was there. When I stopped and shook hands with Spencer, he looked at me sort of funny.

"Are you all right, George?" he asked.

I said, "What do you mean? Of course I'm all right. Don't I look all right?"

He said, "I think you should go to your office and sit down for a minute, George. You look like something is wrong with you. Are you sure you're all right?"

"Spencer," I said, "I feel fine. I don't have to come up here to have people tell me I don't look good. There are plenty of folks in this town who would do that at the drop of a hat. Listen to me. I'm fine." Then I went on to my office, but Spencer came back with me and said, "George, let me call your doctor and see if I can get him to come up here."

I said, "What in the world are you talking about, Spencer?" By this time he noticed that there was a little bit of drawing on the left side of my face. My left eye and my mouth were pulled up a little bit, and I seemed to be losing control of my facial muscles. So he persisted, and even when I refused to listen to him, Spencer insisted on calling my doctor.

> "We've got to get him to the hospital right now. The sooner the better."

He went to the next room and made the call and said, "Something is wrong with George." When the doctor heard my symptoms, he said, "Bring him down to the hospital, Spencer, and I'll see him when you get here."

Spencer came in and told me what was happening, and he said he was going to take me to the hospital. I said, "Spencer, get out of here. Are you nuts? I'm not going to the hospital. There are people out there waiting on me for lunch, and I feel fine." At that time I didn't actually feel any pain, no headaches or anything of that sort. Other than the fact that I had felt weak and sweaty in the car, I didn't think I had any problems. The momentary weakness had already passed. In short, I wasn't very cooperative.

Spencer called the doctor back and tried to get him to come to the office. But the doctor said he couldn't leave the hospital, so at that point Spencer called our trainer, Terry Kofler, and got him to come up to my office. I don't remember seeing Terry come in, but I remember lying down on the couch in my office before he got there, which I never do, not even for a nap. And I promptly fell asleep.

When Terry came in, he took one look at me and said, "We've got to get him to the hospital right now. The sooner the better." The next thing I remember was Spencer lifting me up and saying, "We're going to take you down to the hospital, George."

I said, "Well, let me go to the bathroom first." So I walked down the hall to the bathroom, and when I came back, Spencer and Terry knew for certain that something serious had happened to me. Spencer told me later, "When I saw you then, I knew we had to get you to the hospital. You are always so particular about the way you look, but when you came back from the men's room, you had your tie tucked in your pants and your shirttail was hanging out. You would never come back looking like that ordinarily. The minute I saw you, I knew for certain that something was not quite right."

Winning Big

They drove me to the hospital, and from that moment on my memory is totally blank. I don't remember anything that happened for the next two weeks. As soon as the doctors examined me, they could see that I had suffered a stroke. Dr. Craig Vandermere, the neurologist who treated me, moved me to another hospital and put me in intensive care, and they immediately began giving me medication and treatment for my condition.

They didn't operate on me, exactly. They just drilled a hole in my head and drained off the blood that had pooled around my brain. In time, the wound healed itself. Sometimes when I tell about the experience, I say that the doctors told me that I would recover completely, but my wife isn't so sure. She teases me that I have permanent brain damage!

Later, after I got out of the hospital, they showed me some newspaper clippings from that time. One of the photographs shows me on a stretcher, being transported between hospitals. It looked so foreign to me. I couldn't believe it had happened. I didn't remember anything about it. Even though my eyes were open, I have no memory of that incident. My wife tells me I carried on conversations and greeted visitors the whole time I was in the hospital. I was never unconscious. I even talked about the team and asked how they were doing. But I remember none of that today.

After I had been in the hospital for a couple of weeks, my memory started coming back. The first thing I remember is seeing all those tubes going in and out of my body—to my head, my arms, and everywhere. There were IVs in one arm and a catheter. I thought to myself, *What in the world am I doing here?*

When the nurse came in, the first question I asked was, "Did the Hornets win last night?"

She said, "The Hornets didn't play last night, Mr. Shinn."

I said, "Are you crazy? We sure did. We played the Clippers."

"No, sir. You played the Clippers two weeks ago."

"Two weeks ago?" I gasped. "You've got to be kidding! Did we win?"

She smiled at me and said, "Yes, Mr. Shinn, you did. You won big!" And I'm told I beamed from head to toe when she said that. We only won by one point, but you see, that was the first win in the history of the Charlotte Hornets organization. It couldn't have been any bigger for me.

I suppose it's ironic—after all I had been through and after all my associates and I had done to acquire the team, build the franchise, sell the tickets, and get us to that point—that I would miss our first big win. But I could not be any prouder of the victory if I had been there for the whole game. Later, the team autographed the game ball for me, and you can bet I keep it in a very special place in my home.

When the surgeon came in to see me later that morning, I asked, "Doctor, what happened to me?"

"You had a stroke," he said.

"A stroke?" I couldn't believe it. "You've got to be kidding. Are you sure?"

He said, "Look, I'm a neurologist. I treat people who have strokes and other kinds of brain disorders. Mr. Shinn, there is no doubt that you had a stroke."

"But I can't believe it," I said. "Just this morning—I mean, the morning I had the stroke—I ran five miles. I've been doing that for at least five years. Doctor, I run a hundred miles a month, and I'm in great physical condition. I've never had high blood pressure, I'm not overweight, I don't smoke. I just find it hard to believe I could have a stroke!"

> "You're lucky it happened the way it did and that the people who work for you were alert enough to get you to the hospital."

"Mr. Shinn, what happened to you was forming while you were in your mother's womb. It had nothing to do with your diet, how much exercise you were getting, or what condition you were in at that exact moment. It is possible that your healthy lifestyle may have delayed it for a while, but that stroke was inevitable. You're lucky it happened the way it did and that the people who work for you were alert enough to get you to the hospital."

"You mean I could have died?" I asked.

"You're a very lucky man, Mr. Shinn. If this had happened at home and you had just gone to bed to sleep it off, more than likely you would never have woken up. People who have strokes like yours in their sleep usually die before anybody knows that anything has happened.

"But also," he said, "there's no telling what might have happened if the stroke had hit you while you were at the

Coliseum for the basketball game. With all the commotion and excitement around there, and with all the things going on in that arena, you might never have made it here on time or gotten the treatment you needed. You should thank God that you're alive today."

Looking Backward

Well, I have done more than that. I am endlessly grateful to God for allowing me to survive that incident. More than once, as you can imagine, I have expressed my gratitude to Spencer Stolpen for ignoring my rantings and insisting on taking me to the hospital. I am grateful that Terry Kofler recognized my condition right away and helped get me to the emergency room. Had I stayed there and gone to sleep on my office couch, chances are I wouldn't be here today. That stroke has helped me to see a lot of things with new eyes, and I'm grateful for a lot of things today in ways I never was before.

That incident also piqued my curiosity about my father's death when I was eight years old. Dad was just fifty-one at the time, and I had always been led to believe that he died of a heart attack. I began to wonder if there was some connection between what happened to him and what happened to me. After all, even today some people refer to my accident as a heart attack.

As soon as I was able, I checked into my father's medical records, looked back at the burial records and things of that sort, and sure enough, the documents showed that my father died, not of a heart attack, but of a stroke. In fact, I had the same type of stroke my father died of, and at almost the same age. It was a stroke of the right frontal lobe.

That discovery helped me put some other things in perspective, and in some ways it helped give me a better understanding of my past. Somewhere deep down, I think I probably blamed my father for what happened to our family. If he hadn't died, we wouldn't have lost the store or the farm. I wouldn't have had to wear hand-me-down shoes, and I

123

wouldn't have been embarrassed because we were poor. A lot of things would have been different. But now I could understand in a new and deeper way that none of that was his fault.

He had been carrying around a time bomb inside his head, just as I had, and one day it went off and killed him. The same thing could as easily have happened to me, except that, thank God, I was surrounded by people who judged the situation correctly and got me the help I needed.

The only lasting effect I have had from the stroke is the loss of memory during the two weeks I was in the hospital. I don't run the way I used to; I still exercise, but now I prefer a walk-run combination. Also, before the stroke I could rarely take naps during the day. But now it is easier for me to take a catnap, and I don't mind taking a little time off and relaxing when I'm exhausted.

I suppose in some ways the stroke was also part of the motivation for finally selling my schools. We were going through a lot of problems at that time, and I knew I didn't want that kind of pressure. And the article I'd read saying that Peter O'Malley's primary business was the Los Angeles Dodgers had already convinced me that was the way to go. With the help of First Union Bank, I found an interested buyer, sold the schools, and decided to use the proceeds to buy out my partners in the basketball team.

10

Giving Something Back

I'VE been very fortunate in my business ventures to be surrounded by talented people. No matter what business I've been in, I have been able to bring in such capable employees that I could leave town knowing that things would keep going when I was away. That has been a real blessing. I knew I wanted to keep the Hornets as my primary business and concentrate the majority of my time on the team, but I was also willing to back away somewhat and trust my staff to manage the day-to-day affairs.

I was also more interested in spending time with my family after my stroke. I've always had a good relationship with my wife and kids, so it wasn't a radical change, but we grew closer after that. For one thing, I think maybe my family realized how close they had come to losing me, which was something none of us had thought much about up to that time. Over a period of time, we began spending more time together and enjoying our family time.

Business had always come first in my life. My youngest son was involved in sports, and I tried not to miss any of his games, but basketball is pretty much a night sport, and there were a lot of evenings away from home. Today, my family and I may just decide to fly to Colorado for a few days and go skiing, or we may jump on the plane and go somewhere spontaneously. There are always telephones out there if I need to call somebody. There's not very much that I can't do just as well from the beach or the mountains as I can in Charlotte. But out there I can be with my family full time.

Essential Values

The stroke helped me see all kinds of relationships with new eyes—business, family, and civic obligations. It made me more willing to back away from the daily grind and not be quite so intense about every little detail. But it has also had an impact on my faith and my attitudes about the important things—the essential values.

Sometimes it's only when you find out that you really are mortal that reality sets in. I think I came to that realization after my two weeks in intensive care, when I discovered how close I had come to death. Thinking about that made me want to thank God for not letting this thing be fatal and for giving me an opportunity to continue on with my life.

I've learned that once you get people who have the talent to carry out the job, you can take life a little easier. And if you have trust in those people, then it's a good idea to get out of the way now and then and just let them do it. Loyalty really means a lot to me. Loyalty is critical in any type of business, as it is in life. Whether it's in church, in clubs, or in any other organization, you have to develop a sense of loyalty to the

126

cause. And in most cases your loyalty will be to the organization's leaders.

But loyalty is expressed in other ways too. I'm a firm believer that if you work for somebody and they are paying your wages, it is your duty to give them the best you can at all times. You shouldn't run the business down. Always lift it up, and if for some reason you see something you can't live with, then leave. If for some reason you feel you've been mistreated, leave. Or if for some reason you don't want to be there anymore, leave. But if you're there and you're taking their money, then give them every bit of the time and loyalty and service they're paying you for. And if you do that, it will pay you back tenfold.

I realized that I still had a lot of goals to accomplish in my life, and the awareness of my mortality gave me a new sense of motivation. Simplicity became a goal after that, and that's when I took the suggestion of my advisers that I go ahead and sell all my schools and exercise my option to buy out my partners in the Hornets ownership group. They said, "By the terms of your agreement, George, you have the right to exercise your call option at your own discretion, so we propose that you go ahead and begin that process now."

> *If you work for somebody and they are paying your wages, it is your duty to give them the best you can at all times.*

I contacted my partners and told them what I wanted to do. Felix Sabates didn't want to sell his interest. I reminded him of our agreement and asked him what it would take to make him change his mind. He asked that I pay him back at the rate of two and a half times the amount of his initial investment. Even though I was under no legal obligation to do that, I agreed to his terms and asked my lawyers and accountants to settle up with him.

At that point, I contacted Rick Hendrick and Cy Bahakel and told them I would extend the same offer to each of them.

Rick was surprised. "You don't have to do that, George," he said. "I don't have a problem with our original agreement. We have a legal contract, and all you're obligated to do is repay my original investment with interest, and that will be fine with me." I appreciated his spirit of cooperation, but I said, "Rick, if I'm going to pay Felix the higher amount, then I want to do the same for you. I wouldn't be content doing any less for you and Cy than I am doing for Felix, so that's what I'd like it to be."

So Rick and Felix agreed and settled right away, but suddenly Cy Bahakel didn't want to sign, and before all was said and done, we had to go to court to resolve the matter. Despite our protracted disagreements, I still consider Cy a friend, and I am very grateful for what he, Felix, and Rick did to help make the Charlotte Hornets a reality. There are times when people in business have to defend their interests or take a stand for some particular policy or practice, but if they're truly professionals, they can remain friends through it all. I'm glad to say that I still see each of these men often, and Cy and I get together to play golf several times a year.

Trying to Make a Difference

I still have dreams. I would still like to own a Major League Baseball team one of these days—that was my original goal. I have already looked at ownership possibilities with the San Francisco Giants, the Pittsburgh Pirates, and other teams, but if I do get involved, it will have to make good business and financial sense for me. The 1994–95 strike season changed the perspectives on baseball for a lot of people, and even some owners are wondering about the wisdom of carrying such a large financial risk. But I haven't given up on the idea.

128

When I brought the Hornets to Charlotte, there was only a slight chance that an NBA team could make it here. What we have done over the last seven or eight years is to help transform the marketplace so that now the Carolinas have become a major sports center. My goal, as far as baseball is concerned, would be to have a team where there is already an existing franchise and where there is a marketplace that can support a major league team. The Dodgers would be my dream team, of course, but that is probably not a realistic goal. I'm keeping my eyes open for other possibilities.

The markets that are going to become available for acquisition will be those where the current management has failed for whatever reasons, and most likely a new owner won't be walking into a winning situation. There are risks in that, and you would have to anticipate some major financial liabilities, but that actually motivates me. I believe in my ability to build on a team's traditions and turn things around. That was one reason I was seriously interested in becoming involved with the Pittsburgh Pirates.

But whether it's the Pirates or another team, I will pursue the one that makes the best sense for me at the time, from a business and a personal point of view. We may not want another expansion team in Charlotte at that time. I did pursue it recently, and we didn't make the cut. But there were so many factors involved that I hesitate to base any future plans on that experience. It is costly and very draining to go through that process and then be turned down, so I am not expending any more effort in that direction right now.

> **If your heart is in the right place and if you're really committed to something, then you can live with criticism.**

When you start losing money in Major League Baseball, you lose it fast, and trying to fill a forty-thousand-seat stadium four or five times a week can be a monumental challenge, especially if you have to carry a losing team for the first few years. So those are things I have had to think about the past couple of years.

I still face criticism from some sectors about the basketball team, about our season rankings, or about the coliseum. But I know enough about people to know that if your heart is in the right place and if you're really committed to something, then you can live with criticism. There are critics when you fail and critics when you succeed. There are always some people whose self-appointed task is to start rumors and to sneer; that is just the way it goes. You have to live with a certain amount of criticism.

I don't speak as often as I used to, but I continue to get requests of all kinds, and I have received a number of honors and awards for which I am very grateful. I never went to a university, yet I have six honorary doctorates. I have never had any great academic ambitions, but I serve on the board of a college where I am needed and where I have been able to do some good. And that's my real objective: to motivate people to be the best they can be.

Hardships and Reality

Being involved with Barber-Scotia College has given me many new opportunities to serve, and it has been a very rewarding experience. Because of my own struggles in overcoming financial and educational hardships, I have a sense of kinship with these students. I had to struggle economically and academically for years, so I have a sense of what some African American students have been through. I have seen those struggles from both sides, and I know what it's like to overcome long odds and get ahead.

It was when we started our recruiting programs in the proprietary schools that I first had the chance to reach out to minority students, and I got to know some of their problems firsthand. I learned years ago about problems that most teachers and administrators around this country are only now having to cope with.

Sometimes it is hard for teachers to relate to students who come out of deprived backgrounds. When they have students in their classes who fall asleep or won't study, they don't know how to talk to them about their problems. They just give up on them or give them a failing grade. Sometimes it's hard for teachers to understand what the problems are because they themselves have never experienced anything like that. But that was an experience I understood. I knew exactly what they were going through. I had been there myself.

Some of these kids are coming to school straight from their jobs or from homes without suitable sanitary conditions. Many of them have only one parent, and some have no parents at all. And some who have parents are regularly beaten, abused, intellectually and emotionally deprived, and drained of hope.

A lot of these kids come to school and eat lunch in the cafeteria, and that is the only meal they will have all day. When they fall asleep in the classroom, you don't chew them out or just ignore them: first, you talk to them; then you help them to understand the importance of the opportunity they've been given. Wake them up and motivate them to learn.

I was greeted with the same kind of abuse many of them have experienced.

These kids have really struggled, and they have had their backs against the wall. When I went to Barber-Scotia College for the first meeting after I was appointed board chairman, I was greeted with the same kind of abuse many of them have experienced. There were no boos or disturbances when I was introduced in the assembly, but there were no fanfares either.

Perhaps one example will indicate some of the emotions that came to the surface. When I finished my address, I went out a side door toward the parking lot, and on the way we passed near a small group of students. As we approached, one young black woman walked over to me and, using a racial slur, told us to leave. "We don't want you or your money here!" she said.

I was walking with Roger Schweickert, a former FBI agent who is a key executive with the Hornets. Roger is big and strong as an ox, so I knew I was in no personal danger, but I was shocked, nevertheless. Roger said, "Thank you very much for that warm reception," and we walked on. I couldn't get that incident out of my mind for several days. I eventually realized that I had been given the opportunity to experience a type of anger and hostility that many of the students on that campus have experienced all their lives. Suddenly I knew what it was to be hated simply because of the color of my skin. In some ways it was a good experience for me. There are a lot of blacks who continue to feel as she did, but I believed I could rise above it. I was convinced that the students, faculty, and administrators at Barber-Scotia College needed me and that I was about the only person who was willing to try. I had the substance, the resources, and the connections to do some good. And besides, I wanted to do it.

They may call me names, but when all is said and done, I hope they'll come back to me and say, "Good job, George. We appreciate what you've done." Then I'll move on. As I have said, I do feel a kinship with black students and their circumstances, because I have been in a similar place. And I am interested in helping young people, because I know how much a helping hand can mean. Had it not been for people reaching out to help guide and motivate me, I wouldn't be here today.

Reaching Out to Others

I have always believed that it is important for people who have the ability to help others to do so, and I also believe that whatever you give in faith you will get back tenfold. Some people call this *reciprocity,* which is a big word that means you receive blessings in your life according to how you bless other people. I have always believed that, and I not only teach it but I try to practice it as well. There is enormous satisfaction in reaching out to help others.

I get a lot of personal satisfaction from giving, and it has always come back to reward me in many ways over the years. Sometimes it has helped me financially; sometimes it has just been the personal satisfaction of knowing that I am doing something worthwhile. When I first started making money, I decided I wanted to use my resources to help other people and other organizations, so, as I mentioned earlier, I established the George Shinn Foundation.

Pat Clayton, who was a partner at Arthur Andersen and a financial adviser at that time, suggested that a foundation would be the best way for my family and me to make donations to worthy causes. At the same time, a well-organized foundation would help to protect the funds I had set aside for that purpose. Pat, who is a strong Christian and a devoted church member, was serving as treasurer of his church at the time. When I told him of my plan to give 10 percent of my income to Christian charities and other benevolent causes, he told me about the options available through a foundation and suggested I do it that way.

"I know how you feel about giving," Pat told me, "and I appreciate your desire to give money to your church, but as an investment adviser, I strongly recommend that you set up a foundation to manage your contributions. When you just pick and choose places to make donations at random, there is no discipline to your giving. That can be a disadvantage for the organizations you support.

"What you might consider," he said, "is setting up a foundation with a board of directors or perhaps a part-time administrator to help decide on the best uses of that money. You can bless a lot more people over the years if you do it that way."

Pat's suggestion made a lot of sense to me, so that's what we did. Today, the Shinn Foundation is a nonprofit corporation that handles most of my charitable donations. I don't always put the money directly into the foundation. If I come across a special need or if I decide to recognize a particularly worthy enterprise, I may write a check on the spot. It depends on whether or not we agree that the foundation is the best way to make the gift. Whether it is a gift from the Charlotte Hornets, from Shinn Enterprises, or from our personal account, Carolyn and I take great pleasure in the privilege of using our blessings to bless and encourage others.

In the beginning we wanted to put together a board to help us decide how to use the money. However, I found out very quickly that each member of the board had his own agenda and his own list of worthy causes. They weren't as interested in my giving priorities as they were in their own. When I saw what was happening, I went to my minister and said, "Do you know someone who would like to work part time running a foundation for me and helping me give away my money the way that I would like to do it?"

He said he thought he knew someone, and he arranged a luncheon meeting. A few days later we got together with Mr. C. L. Jenkins, a retired businessman and a member of our church, and I explained what I had in mind. He asked me a couple of exploratory questions, and then he said he would be honored to have such a job. If I decided to hire him, he said, he would make sure that my wishes were followed to the letter. So, before we finished our meal that day, Mr. Jenkins became the first director of the Shinn Foundation.

> **Each member of the board had his own agenda and his own list of worthy causes.**

Mr. Jenkins—my family and I began calling him Jenk—was one of the most down-to-earth guys I had ever met. His wife of many years had died of cancer a few years earlier, and their three children were all very successful in their lives and careers. His son Joe was a physician and an attorney, and C. L. Jenkins, Jr., earned his Ph.D. and went on to become president of St. Mary's College in Raleigh.

Jenk was a guy who held the same beliefs and views as Carolyn and I, and he was committed to doing things the right way. He always kept me informed of what was happening, and he would give me his guidance and recommendations about various charitable causes. He told me, "I would never want to take advantage of you or your money, George.

134

East & West All-Stars warming up prior to 1991 NBA All-Star Game in Charlotte.

1992: Players & coaches discuss strategy during a time-out.

Muggsy and LJ celebrate during a playoff game vs. the Celtics in 1

Former Hornet Armon Gilliam signing autographs prior to a Hornets game.

Scott Burrell during practic

Muggsy and LJ on the bench during a Hornets game.

View from above of Hornets trying to stop Shaq.

Above: George with Alonzo Mourning at a press conference after he was signed to a contract.

Below: George and Larry Johnson participating in a Hornets postgame radio interview following a playoff victory.

Below: The HoneyBees, the newly selected Hornets dance team, pose for a picture with George.

Above: Hugo, the Hornets mascot.

Below: Hugo's alter ego, Super Hugo, dazzles fans with one of his acrobatic dunks.

Above: George Shinn and Allan Bristow riding in a downtown parade put on by the city after the team completed its first playoff appearance.

Below: Allan Bristow and Spencer Stolpen celebrate the Hornets' luck in winning the NBA lottery and getting to select first in the 1991 NBA draft. (The pick was used to select Larry Johnson.)

Below: For George's fiftieth birthday, he received one of his cars redone with a Hornets motif.

Alonzo Mourning and Kendall Gill at a dedication ceremony for one of the many basketball courts the Hornets have refurbished throughout Charlotte's lower-income areas. Some courts were painted by the Hornets and dedicated in memory of two police officers who were killed on duty in the area.

George giving away brand-new bicycles to over one hundred underprivileged kids and throwing them a Christmas party.

Residents of the George Shinn Homeless Shelter having a meal. Following the meal, each resident was given a pair of boots for Christmas, donated by George.

George congratulating a young lady who had just been notified she
would be a HoneyBee for the coming Hornets season.

George and Carolyn Shinn at the Hornets' first regular-season home game at the Charlotte Coliseum,
November 4, 1988. Everyone was encouraged to wear tuxedos that night.

The 1990–91 team poster.

CHARLOTTE HORNETS
1991-92

NBA

ATTENDANCE CHAMPIONS
971,618

One of the many attendance-champion banners that
hang from the rafters at the Charlotte Coliseum.

I realize where this money comes from, and I am not interested in what other people may want me to do with your money. Ultimately, it's your decision, and we will put the money where you feel it will do the most good." So he impressed me early on.

Over a period of time, Jenk practically became my children's adopted grandfather. He often traveled with my family and me, and he was everything from baby-sitter to counselor to spiritual adviser. Not only did Carolyn and I love him, but our children loved him too, and everybody who worked for us loved him. In many ways he was like a father to me. Jenk is in his eighties now, and a couple of years back he moved to a retirement home in the area. He remains a much-loved friend of the family and the person who did more than anyone to help me design and shape my philosophy of giving.

Jenk still tells the story about the first time we met and how I brought him on board. "When George hired me to run the foundation, he said it was going to be a part-time job," he says, "but he never told me which twelve hours it was supposed to be!" And he says, "I have worked for George half a day ever since, twelve hours in the morning some days, twelve hours in the evening some days." He's probably right. Until his re-retirement, he was my golfing buddy and spiritual mentor, and we never had a meeting that he didn't begin the discussion with prayer. He was just what I needed at that particular time in my life.

That They Might Lead

At one point Jenk told me about a small Bible college in the mountains near Asheville, in Henderson, North Carolina, called Fruitland Bible Institute. It was supported by the Southern Baptist Convention, but just marginally. At Jenk's urging, I went up to visit the school and see their situation. That was one of the most enlightening and uplifting times I have ever experienced. Here we were, talking to young people who were fully committed to preaching and teaching the Bible but with almost no money to complete their educations.

Some of their stories were incredible. It would bring a man to his knees to hear what some of those young people had gone through to pursue their dream of teaching the Word. Some had lost everything but their faith. Some were living on next to nothing. Some didn't even own a change of clothes. So we made a commitment to help them out by donating a certain amount of money for scholarships each year, and Mr. Jenkins conducted those interviews.

There is a lot of red tape and IRS regulations to go through in these kinds of situations, so we had to prepare for that as well. Mr. Jenkins took care of all that, and then he would go up and interview the students each quarter. He often said that sometimes the experience would lift him up so much it would carry him the rest of the year. Some of the scholarships might be for no more than $100 while others might be for the full amount of the tuition. It depended on the actual needs of the students. I gave Jenk the authority to make those decisions on his own.

> It would bring a man to his knees to hear what some of those young people had gone through to pursue their dream of teaching the Word.

At the end of the year, we would put on a Christmas party for them. We sent a bus up to get the students and bring them down to Charlotte for a celebration. We put them up for the night; then we had a special dinner at the church. Most of the students lived at or near the poverty level, so we would also collect clothes donated by our church and the local community and give them to anyone who needed them.

On Sunday morning they would all come to church with us. Most of the time our church is fairly quiet and formal, but not on those days. You would hear amens all over the sanctuary, and those students just sang their hearts out. Everybody looked forward to those Sundays, because it made us feel so good to know that we were helping people who needed it so badly—people who were completely dedicated to serving the Lord through a career in the ministry. And I think our minister loved those times most of all.

For a while I was on the board of Southeastern Seminary in Wake Forest, North Carolina, which is the site of the original Wake Forest College. As a result of my relationship there, I agreed to give them a fairly substantial amount each year for their scholarship fund. They had originally wanted it to be an endowment, but I preferred to make direct gifts to deserving students. Instead of using just the interest on my gift and helping one or two students, I would rather see the money go to help twenty people. In other words, instead of giving one or two $1,000 scholarships per year, I preferred to give twenty $1,000 scholarships. So that's what we did.

After my stroke I began to take all these matters more seriously. It wasn't because I wanted to be seen as a philanthropist or a good guy, and I certainly didn't think that giving to others would gain me any special privileges or favors. What I realized was that we each have a brief moment to use our gifts, our time, our talent, and our money to help other people. There isn't a minute to waste. I always tried to give to others whenever I thought of it, but occasional off-the-cuff giving was simply not enough, and that's why I have formalized the process.

Today, I contribute to the maintenance and upkeep of the men's shelter in Charlotte. I am a big fan and supporter of the Boy Scouts, and I like to do whatever I can to help the schools in our area, and those are ongoing, year-round concerns. I have countless other interests, but the object is to do whatever I can, while I still can, to make the world a better place. I have seen how quickly life can change, and that's one of the main reasons I am committed to making a difference with the time and resources I have.

11
Learning to Believe

WHEN I wrote my book *The Miracle of Motivation,* I said that the first and most important step in learning to have faith is learning to believe in yourself. Believing is not an action but an attitude. It involves your deepest feelings and emotions.

When you really believe in something, you have confidence in it, and you think it has value—whether it is another person, an idea, or a principle of faith. And to really believe in anything, you first have to believe in yourself, because you can't hold positive feelings of acceptance and trust for anything until you first have trust and acceptance for yourself.

During my growing-up years I discovered that self-confidence was the most important part of believing. To have the kind of faith my mother encouraged me to have, I had to learn how to believe in myself, and that wasn't always easy. Of course, I understood that faith and reverence were important. But it wasn't until my attitudes about who I am began to change, and until I began to see that I could make something of myself, that I was able to understand very much about faith.

So many young people today don't seem to have very much self-respect. They don't trust themselves. They don't think they can get ahead in life, and they're afraid of what might happen to them in the future. How can they believe in anything when they feel so hopeless and helpless? As I have said, I didn't always feel good about myself. Every time I messed up in school or disappointed my mother or my teachers, I felt really bad. I'm sure that at times I wondered if I would ever amount to anything. But one day I began to trust myself, to take more chances, and to do things in the simple belief that if I worked hard and did my best, everything would work out fine. Most of the time, it did.

Many people know that we always have a prayer before each Charlotte Hornets game. We do that for a couple of reasons. First, we do it to fulfill a personal commitment I made to honor the Lord, because he was always there to help me along the way. But second, we do it because we all need faith in our lives. Prayer is a way of reaching out to God. It is a way of showing that we believe there is a need for faith and hope, and that there is always a way through your difficult circumstances. We want to recognize those and other important values that can only come through faith.

Oddly enough, the Hornets is still the only team in all of professional sports that does that, and the reason we do it has never been fully articulated in the media. I have repeated my mother's words several times, that if we have the faith, God has the power. Well, I had the faith. I believed that I could bring a professional basketball team to North Carolina. I believed that getting the team was going to benefit the community. I also believed that it was going to be successful and profitable, and God has allowed all of those things to come true.

Knowing When to Pray

I have never considered myself to be a religious leader or anything of that sort. I certainly don't see myself in that role. But I do feel that after all God has done for me, the least I can do is show him the respect he deserves and acknowledge his part in giving us this team. Without God's guidance, along with the power he has given me, we would never have made it to where we are today.

I can remember times when I would get up in the morning and read the newspaper, and it was so full of bad news and discouraging words that I could have easily become depressed. But somehow I was able to rise above it and go on to pursue my dreams and goals. You know, going back to the roots of both the Lord's promise and the promise my mom gave me was the most important step I ever took. I be-

Along the way I was told that I couldn't have an opening prayer.

lieved that if I had faith and if I pushed toward my dreams, God would help me achieve those dreams. That thought has been in the back of my mind my entire life, and it has influenced and directed all my successes.

When I first decided to begin each basketball game with a short prayer, I called my minister, Rev. Henry Crouch, and asked if he would be the chaplain for the Hornets. In addition to giving a short devotional for our players and staff before each game, I wanted him to help me get a different minister, priest, or rabbi to pray at the start of the game. Henry didn't hesitate. He said yes to all of the above. But along the way I was told that I couldn't have an opening prayer. Our general manager at that time, Carl Sheer, told me I shouldn't do it.

"What do you mean?" I said. "Why shouldn't we have a

short prayer before the game? That has been part of my plans from the very beginning."

Carl said, "There's not another team in the league that does it, George."

"Are you serious? I'm sure one or two teams have a prayer before their games, don't they?"

"No, they don't."

I was disappointed and upset by the news. After thinking about it, I decided not to have the prayer. Norm Sonju, general manager of the Dallas Mavericks, had suggested that we might want to have a prayer on opening night. Even though that wasn't quite the same thing, I decided to settle for it.

I called Henry Crouch at home and told him what I had learned. I said, "Well, Henry, it looks like we can't have the prayer, so I'd appreciate it if you would call—"

Henry interrupted me. "George, I have already called all those ministers and lined everything up."

"I know, Henry," I said. "I'm sorry, but you'll just have to call them all back and tell them we're not going to do it."

I couldn't sleep that night. The decision not to have a prayer was heavy on my mind. I felt like I was letting down my strongest source of strength. I was letting him down by not honoring a plan that I had been thinking about since the very beginning. I didn't exactly *promise* God that I was going to have a prayer—I hadn't gone quite that far. But it was definitely in the back of my mind, in my thoughts, and God knows our thoughts.

So after a sleepless night, I called Henry back and said, "Henry, I'm sorry, but I have changed my mind again. We are going to have that prayer before each game, and we'll just keep on doing it until they make us stop. I'm embarrassed to put you to so much trouble, Henry, but I guess you'll just have to call all those preachers back and reschedule them."

Henry laughed and said, "That's great, George. I never canceled them to begin with. I knew you'd come through!"

Faith and Values

I talked first with the people in the league office and told them what we were going to do, and that's how we got started. I wasn't apologetic or hesitant about it. I just wanted to make sure that we did it in a way that would be open and aboveboard, and with no surprises.

I told them it was going to be a nondenominational, nonsectarian prayer so that nobody would be offended, and I also said that we were going to do it before the television cameras came on. TV airtime is very expensive, and if we stopped and asked everybody to bow their heads for a moment of prayer while the cameras were running, the guys at the networks wouldn't be very happy. We planned to have the prayer early so it wouldn't affect the TV programming.

> It sends a signal to people that we have a good organization here that cares about the deeper things.

In addition to the pregame prayer, we also have a brief chapel service before every game. We invite not only our players and employees to come, but also any members of the opposing team who want to take part. A sign is posted in the opponents' locker room telling them when the chapel service will be held. You would be surprised at how many opposing players come to the chapel service.

The speakers offer a different message at each chapel, which includes a ten-minute devotional and a prayer. That's all there is to it, but it is really refreshing to have that time. I also think it sends a signal to people that we have a good organization here that cares about the deeper things. Many players really appreciate the fact that we have a chapel service. No matter what denomination or religion a person may be, they know that there is more than just flash and sparkle and big-time sports going on here. We care about faith and values, and we're not afraid to show it.

Another thing we do that I have never seen other sports franchises do is that during the national anthem our players all salute the flag. They put their hands over their hearts. I have never seen another team do it, but I asked our players to and they agreed. Just in case there was anyone who might be hesitant, I told them, "You know, I don't ask a lot of things of you men, but I am very proud to be an American. I'm proud of my heritage. I'm proud of this country, and I am a beneficiary of this system. I am living proof that the American Dream still works, and so are all of you guys.

"You men are among the highest-paid people not just in this city but in the entire world. And if anybody should be proud of this system and salute it," I said, "it should be you."

All our players do salute the flag today, and I believe they are all happy to do it. One of the best pictures I have of our team is one somebody took of the guys out on the court, standing together side by side and saluting the flag. I have that picture framed, hanging over my desk, and it means as much to me as anything I own. There's not another team that does either of those things. We're the only team that has a pregame prayer, and we're the only one whose players all salute the American flag, and that makes me proud.

Other people notice what we're doing, and apparently it makes them proud too. As just one example, there was a letter to the editor in a New York newspaper the week of May 27, 1995, written by a businessman who said he was tired of going to sporting events where there was total disrespect for the national anthem by both players and fans. When he was in Charlotte on business, he went to a Hornets game. What a refreshing thing it was, he said, to go to a basketball game opened by an invocation followed by the national anthem, during which the fans all stood up and the players put their hands on their hearts. He said it gave him a breath of hope that people weren't all as bad as he sometimes thought. We are always pleased to get that kind of positive feedback, and we're glad to see that people from other cities are watching what we do. It just reinforces my belief that character counts.

Successful Living

When I'm speaking to an audience, I try to get across three simple points on living life successfully. The first is to *concentrate on good health*. Take care of your body; take care of yourself. The second is that *you've got to have a good attitude*. Think positive thoughts. If you look for bad things to come, they are going to come. If you look for good things, good things will come your way. That's not my idea; it's a biblical concept, and that's the way God intended for this life to be. And the third principle, to me, is the foundation of all the rest, and that is to *have faith*.

Faith in God is key, of course. But beyond that, we also need to have faith in this country. Even with all the problems we have, this is still the greatest place in the world to live. People from Cuba, Haiti, Mexico, and South America are risking their lives every day just to come here. All over the world people dream of coming to America—the land of the free. We should be proud of this great country. This is the only place in the world where a guy who graduated last in his class could set a goal of owning a major league team and actually reach that goal. That only works in America. So be proud of it. Support this system because it works. Have faith in it.

You've also got to have faith in people. People are what make other people great. You've got to believe in folks. You've got to trust them. Had it not been for people in this community, there's no way that I could ever have accomplished my goals. The people in this community trusted me. They believed in me, had faith in me, and lifted me up beyond my highest expectations. I didn't do that; the people here did that for me. And I realize that without them I would have nothing today. I mean, it's that simple. I also tell people that when you get down to the personal level, the biggest disappointments in life are people when they let you down. It is not things or situations or fate that disappoints us but people, and unfortunately those disappointments usually come from those who are very close to us—the ones we love the most. But the lesson of faith is that we have to overlook those hurts and keep on loving others.

If someone hurts you with their words or actions, don't compound the problem by trying to get even. Continue to love them, continue to trust them, and continue to have faith in them. That is a biblical principle. Show faith in others whether they deserve it or not. And if you truly have faith in other people, I believe they will repay your faith. Have faith in them and people will lift you up. The more people you have loving you and the more people you have lifting you up, the higher you go.

Essential Truths

Whenever I speak about faith, it is usually to diverse groups with a broad mixture of people in the audience. I always try to get the point across that God created all of us: men, women, and children of every race and tribe. God made each one of us special, and we can all do something. We need to have faith in ourselves.

> *God makes no mistakes. And he expects you to be proud to be you.*

Since the beginning of time, billions of people have walked the face of this earth. There has never been and there will never be another you. You are that special. There has never been anybody with your fingerprints, never anybody that looks exactly like you. God made us different shapes, sizes, and colors, but he made us just the way we are, and he makes no mistakes. And he expects you to be proud to be you. It's that simple.

You've got to have faith in you, and you've got to beat your own drum. You've got to go after it. You've got to have faith that you were put here to be the best you that you can be. Don't ever pull yourself down by thinking negative thoughts. God made you, and you insult him when you run yourself down. When you say, "I'm too fat, I'm too this, or I'm too that," you cheapen your own value. Hold yourself up, believe in yourself, and have faith in yourself.

You know, I believe in those things. If I could change myself, I would probably be taller. But God made me short, and God makes no mistakes. So I'm proud to be me, and you should be proud to be you, whoever and wherever you are. You show reverence to God when you show that you are proud of yourself. Keep a smile on your face, think positive thoughts, be proud to be who you are, and have faith in others. Have faith in the system, in yourself, and in God.

Like most people, I have made a lot of mistakes during my lifetime. I have made bad decisions, messed up, and had to start over more than once. But with all the mistakes and problems I've had, and despite fears and uncertainties at times, I have learned in my fifty years of life that the greatest source of strength known to man is a mere human being who is willing to get down on his knees and ask God for guidance.

Someone has said that prayer changes things, and I truly believe that. It can change physical circumstances in some cases, but it can also change you from the inside out, and that may be the biggest change of all. We are never stronger than when we kneel before God in prayer, and we're never weaker than when we think we can just keep plowing ahead blindly in our own strength, believing that whatever happens will be good enough. It's never too late to start—and it's always too soon to give up hope.

Furthermore, it's never too late to start over, but it's always too soon to start doubting yourself and your dreams.

A Sense of Perspective

When I look back over the past fifty years, I can see that a lot of my success came because I didn't know I couldn't succeed in some of the things I tried to do. If I had been better educated or more informed on some of those things, I might have doubted myself and given up before I even started. But since nobody told me it was impossible, I just went ahead and did it. I'm sure there were plenty of people who would have been glad to tell me how foolish or stupid I was being or that I would be running into brick walls. I didn't hear those people, because I didn't know any better. I just went ahead and fulfilled my dreams the best way I knew how.

I made a comment along those lines one time, saying that I was just God's little idiot. Somebody picked that up, and when it came out in the newspaper the next day, they made it sound a lot worse than I had intended it. I wasn't saying that I'm some kind of bumpkin or that God felt sorry for me and let me have some success in life. All I was saying was that it doesn't take the smartest guy in the world to be successful in business or anywhere else. We can all be "successful" if we turn off the negative messages that the world gives us—and that we give to ourselves so much of the time—and just do the best we can with the equipment we have.

Somebody asked me once if I was surprised at what I have been able to accomplish in my life. The reporter who asked the question was a little bit rude, and I recall that my answer was pretty direct. "No, I'm not surprised at all," I said. "I'm where I am today because a number of years ago I planned to be here."

Now, I will be the first to admit that there have been some twists and turns along the way, and I have had some set-backs. But I am not surprised to be in my current position. I set out the plans for my career when I was very young, and I have followed them faithfully step-by-step, trusting in God and putting forth my best effort for each achievement. I believe that it's important for people, no matter where they are in life, to take the time to sit down and put together a plan for their lives—what they hope to accomplish over a lifetime and how they expect to get there. That's a big part of my message to young people today.

When we were first exploring the possibility of getting an NBA franchise, I wanted to learn everything there was to know about running a professional franchise, and I took every chance I could to learn more. During that time the NBA invited prospective owners to come to the All-Star Weekend in Dallas, and I went with great anticipation. I went to every practice, press conference, and seminar I could attend.

On Saturday at one in the afternoon there was a long-distance shoot-out for the top three-point shooters, and that event was to be followed by the slam-dunk contest. I decided to go to the arena early to get a feel for the way things were set up. I wanted to see the advertising, the food-service system, and the menus, as well as the locker rooms, press box, stands, and everything else. If we got a team, we would need to know those things, so I wanted to see it all before the crowds arrived. In fact, I was one of the first people admitted to the arena that morning.

As I was walking around the concourse, making notes and looking things over, I could hear someone dribbling a basketball down on the court. I didn't know if some kid was playing around or what was going on—I was surprised anyone was down there. I went to the court area and looked out from the second-floor stands. I could see someone in a green-and-white uniform shooting baskets. He would shoot, retrieve the rebound, come back to the three-point line, and shoot again. This was at least two hours before the contest was to start, and I was impressed that somebody wanted to win this thing that badly.

> *I could hear someone dribbling a basketball down on the court.*

As it turned out, the shooter was Larry Bird, the legendary forward for the Boston Celtics. Suddenly I understood more about his spirit and commitment, and why he has been described by some sportswriters as one of, if not *the*, greatest to ever play the game. After that I was pulling for Larry in the contest, and as it turned out, he won the shoot-out that year and the next two years. Later, in a conversation with Red Auerbach, the Celtics president, I mentioned that story and he told me that was typical for Larry. He was one of the few superstars who would always take the extra step to work on his game like that and would give himself no excuses for not being the best he could be. That said a lot to me.

149

Knowing How to Score

If you think your back is up against the wall, then make a plan to get out of that situation and get your life on track. First you have to have a goal, a target that is reachable each day, and then work toward those things with real determination. When I was counseling and working closely with the students in our business schools, I always tried to get the point across that you don't become a great basketball player because you're big. You become a great basketball player because you work at it. Even Larry Bird had to work at it, and because he did, he is considered one of the greatest of all time.

Whether it's in sports or business, you first have to make a plan and then put the effort behind the plan. If your goal is to be in the NBA, then part of your plan is to practice. You go out and shoot hoops. It might be raining, but you shoot hoops. The floor you're dribbling the ball on might be broken and uneven, and it might be in terrible condition, and you might not even have a hoop to shoot at, but you keep shooting anyway. You practice, practice, practice. And you have to do what it will take to achieve your goals in a realistic and practical way.

If you live in North Carolina and you want to go to California, you don't just jump in your car and start driving without some kind of plan. If you do, you're sure not going to end up where you want to be. You have to have a map, and you have to mark out your route and plan which way you're going to travel. You'll have to figure out which roads you're going to get on, what cities you will pass through, and where you're going to spend the night. You plan all those things so you'll have a realistic hope of getting to the place where you want to be.

If you don't do that, you have no one to blame but yourself. But if you do, chances are you'll get there quickly and safely. There are many other examples I could give of the same principle. You don't build a house without planning. You don't get a college education without planning. And you'll never earn a million dollars unless you have a plan and a road map showing how you're going to do it.

Why do people try to run their lives without planning? That just doesn't make any sense to me. You've got to have goals. You've got to have purpose in your life. Can you imagine driving to the Charlotte Coliseum for a Hornets game, only to see all the players for both teams come out on the court, with no hoops, no goals, nothing to shoot for? How do you score? You can't hit a target that isn't there!

Without those things it would be a meaningless exercise with nothing to gain. You have to have something to shoot for, and you need to know the rules of the game. You have to have a target, and you have to know how to score. Unfortunately, a lot of people don't consider those basic facts, and as a result they just wander around aimlessly, wondering why they never get ahead in life.

12

The Trouble Tree

SOMETIMES you just have to back away a little bit and put things into perspective so you can see the things that really matter in life. Life from the inside out can be pretty complicated, and before you can make realistic plans, you need to have realistic priorities. Someone I met down in South Carolina a few years ago taught me a valuable lesson about perspective.

My family and I had built a house down at the beach as a retreat from our busy lives in Charlotte. We would go there to relax and play together as a family. There always seemed to be a lot more upkeep and repair work to be done than we would have liked. The house was right on the oceanfront, and after a couple of years we were just overwhelmed at what the elements—the salt air and the general dampness from the sea breezes—would do to a house like that.

One of our biggest problems was that we couldn't find anybody we could trust to come over and do the handiwork for us. I kept searching and searching, and one day somebody recommended a fellow who was good and reliable, and had reasonable prices. Everyone told us he always did a good job and we could trust him. So we decided to give him a try.

I had to have some work done on the front doors on the beach house. They were big double doors, and after just a couple of years the hinges and bolts that go into the wooden frame started to rot out. The doors were literally coming off their hinges. There was also some painting that needed to be done, and the outside lights needed to be replaced, so I called this handyman and asked him to come over and give me an estimate on what it would take to fix things up.

In the meantime, I had measured the doors and gone down to the hardware store and ordered them myself. While I was there, I bought some cheap outdoor lamps and a cheap little ladder. I didn't want to spend much money, but I thought that having these things at the house might be helpful to the handyman, and it would no doubt save him some time.

So this guy came and gave me a price. He was going to do some painting, hang the doors for me, put up some screens, replace some of the light fixtures, and all of the things on my list. He planned to be there the next morning at eight, and he would be all finished up by six that night.

We agreed on a price, and he showed up right on time the next day. I took him into the garage and showed him where everything was, and then I went back upstairs. A short time later I heard an electric saw going down in the garage. I couldn't imagine what in the world he needed to saw, so I wandered back downstairs to take a look. I could see that he was sawing on the doors I had ordered, so I said, "What are you doing?"

He said, "Mr. Shinn, I don't know who ordered these doors for you, but obviously they didn't know what they were doing. They got the wrong size, so I've got to cut a couple inches off to make them fit."

"Well," I said, "I'll talk to the people who messed that up tomorrow." I wasn't about to admit that I did it. I was still too proud for that! So I just went back upstairs while he finished cutting the doors so they would fit. But no sooner had I gotten back to my room than I heard the electric saw stop and heard what sounded like a handsaw down there. I walked back downstairs and said, "What happened?"

> *The ladder looked like it had just gobbled him up.*

He said, "Well, Mr. Shinn, those doors are awful heavy and my electric saw burned up on me. But fortunately I brought my manual saw, and I can cut it just fine with this."

The Problems Never End

The next thing I knew he was downstairs hanging the doors, using my cheap ladder, and all of a sudden I heard this huge crash. I ran downstairs, and there he was, lying on the floor with the door and the ladder all piled up in a heap. My cheap ladder had folded up on him, and he had hit the ground hard, skinning up his elbows and knees and banging the side of his head on the floor. He was wracked up pretty good, and the ladder looked like it had just gobbled him up.

I looked at that pile of destruction and said to myself, *I thought I was doing something to help this guy and keep the cost down, but everything I gave him was either the wrong size or so cheap it just made everything worse. Not only did I not save any money in ordering those things myself, I got the wrong sizes, put a man's life at risk on that ridiculous ladder, and got him hurt in the process.* But before I could say a word, *he* started apologizing to *me*.

"I'm real sorry, Mr. Shinn," he said. "I shouldn't have been so clumsy, and I'm real sorry I messed up your ladder like that."

I said, "Oh no, you don't have to apologize to me. It was my mistake, and I'm the one who should be sorry. This ladder was too weak and too cheap, and I'm sorry for the problems I've caused you."

"Well," he said, "I have a ladder in my truck." And he went down to the truck and got his own ladder and finished the job—just as it started raining.

I couldn't believe it. It was one thing after another. It took him at least an hour longer than he had planned. Since I had already made out the check for the amount we had agreed on, I reached into my pocket and offered him a couple of twenty-dollar bills to make up for the extra time and all the trouble he'd had. He wouldn't take it.

"No, sir, Mr. Shinn," he said. "I agreed on a certain amount and that's all I'll take."

I really respected this man; he was obviously a man of character. I said, "Please take this. It'll make me feel better since I caused you so many problems today." I couldn't quite admit that I had been the one who screwed the doors up, but I said, "Look, I'm the one who bought this cheap ladder that got you hurt. It's my fault, and the least I can do is help cover your expense for all your time and trouble."

He shook his head. "Thank you, Mr. Shinn. I'll just take what you owe me and I'll go." He took the check and started to leave. As I went back to the house, he walked down the path to his ancient old pickup truck, and after a few minutes I heard him out there cranking and cranking the engine. It kept grinding away, but it wouldn't start for anything.

I said, "Oh no, not that too! What else can go wrong?"

After a few minutes there was a knock on the door, and I said, "Oh, man, this guy is going to shoot me!" I tried to get Carolyn to go downstairs and talk to him, but she said, "No, way, Mr. Shinn! You get on down there and talk to him yourself. You're the one who got us into this fix."

So I went downstairs and opened the door. I knew everything had gone wrong, and I felt absolutely awful. But I opened the door and said, "Look, I'm sorry. I see that your truck won't start."

He said, "Yes, sir. I'm having a little problem with it. If it wouldn't be too much trouble, would you mind taking me home? I'll get my brother to bring me back tomorrow, and we'll pick up the truck."

"I would be happy to do that," I said. We got into my car and headed off toward his place. As a motivational speaker, I thought there ought to be something I could say to a guy who had been through all he'd been through. So I tried to tell him that we all have problems in life, we all stumble, we all make mistakes. "You just have to put all that stuff behind you," I said. I was pumping him up like I would an auditorium full of businessmen, trying to cheer up a guy who had just had a terrible day. The only thing he would say was, "Take a right turn at the next intersection," or "Keep going straight past the next stop sign."

I finally realized that the best thing I could do was to keep my mouth shut and take the guy home. I'd say thank you and then go on back to my own house. We finally stopped at his tiny little house, and he said, "Mr. Shinn, would you like to come inside for a second? I would like you to meet my wife and children."

The Light of My Life

"Why, sure," I said, "I would like that." The fact was, I thought the guy had died on the way home. He wouldn't talk to me or respond to anything I said. I was amazed that he would ask me to come in after all that had happened.

There was a little screen porch on the side of the house. Obviously he had built it, and it was just sort of tacked onto the house. We got out and went up to the house. But as I was walking toward the door, I noticed that he had stopped. There was a little tree out in the yard, and he was standing there not saying a word. There was a small branch hanging there, just over his head, and he had reached up and was rubbing the leaves with his fingertips.

To say I was puzzled would be an understatement. I thought, *What in the world is this guy doing? Is this some kind of ritual? What's going on?* I didn't ask him. In fact, I didn't say anything. In a little bit he turned around, and we went up to the door.

He had been calling me Mr. Shinn all day, but the minute he opened the door, he said, "Come on in, George. I want you to meet my family." I followed him into the house, and I could not believe what happened. It was an absolute transformation. I mean, the guy totally changed.

We went into the kitchen, where his wife was cooking dinner. He walked over to her, picked her up, and started swinging her around. They were laughing, and that was one of the most incredible scenes I have ever seen. Now his wife wasn't a small woman, so it must have been quite a tussle to lift her up that way, but he swung her around like nothing at all. When he put her down, he looked over at me and said, "George, this is my wife. This lady is my life. She's not just my wife, she's my life."

> It was an absolute transformation. The guy totally changed.

Then all of a sudden I heard footsteps coming down the hallway, and in came two young teenagers, a boy and a girl. He reached over and threw his arms around them and gave them a great big hug, and he started going on about how great they were. Knowing what all he had been through that day, I just couldn't believe my eyes. In a minute or two I heard more footsteps running down the hall. This time it was three little towheaded kids, all under the age of six, and they were yelling every step of the way, "Daddy, Daddy, Daddy!"

So this big guy got down on his knees, and the kids jumped all over him. One leaped into his arms and the other two were on his back, and he gave them all a big hug and tousled their hair. As soon as things settled down a little bit, he introduced me to each kid, and then he walked over and put his arms around his wife and said, "Well, George, this is my family. Aren't they great? I couldn't do anything without my family and particularly without this little lady here. She's everything to me."

I can't describe my feelings after that experience. I was so humbled by this man and his relationship with his family that you could have swept me up with a broom. We chatted for a few more minutes; then we walked outside and I told everybody good-bye.

Before I got into my car, I looked at this guy and said, "You know, I can't believe what I just witnessed. That was one of the most incredible things I have ever seen. I mean, everything went wrong today over at my house. You burned up your saw, you almost broke your neck on my stupid ladder, you had to do extra work that you weren't getting paid for, your car broke down, and everything that could go wrong did—and besides that, you got rained on! Then you come into this house totally changed. You went from being depressed and frustrated to absolutely joyful and with this incredible zest for life. *What happened?*"

He paused for a moment, then said, "Did you notice right before we went inside the house that I stopped at this little tree here and rubbed the leaves?"

"Yes," I said, "I couldn't help but notice that."

"Well, George," he said, "this here is my trouble tree. Every night when I come home, I usually have all kinds of problems on my mind and all kinds of things that caused trouble for me during the day. But before I go in the house, I just bring all those troubles over here and leave them on this tree. When I go inside to see my wife and kids, I know that my troubles are all outside. I leave them out there all night, you know. And the next morning when I come out, most of them are gone. And the ones that are still there aren't near as big as they were the night before."

I was speechless. All the way from my house I had been trying to give this man a pep talk. Here I was, a motivational speaker with all those good words about how you can overcome your problems, and this big gentle man lays on me one

159

of the most powerful stories of my life. These were simple people. The guy may have had a sixth-grade education at best, but he taught me a lesson I will never forget. He had a trouble tree. That was his secret, and that trouble tree helped him make it through each day, one step at a time.

Do you have a trouble tree?

I do. My "trouble tree" is God. When I see things stacking up and life getting harder, I just pause wherever I am and ask God to help get me through it. He never says no. Sometimes he takes the problems off my shoulders; sometimes he makes them a little easier to bear. We all need a trouble tree. We need to have somewhere to hang our problems so we can sleep at night and so we can give our loved ones the very best part of us.

Going Through It Together

One of the most important reasons for leaving your problems on your trouble tree is so that you can preserve and protect your relationships with the people who matter most in your life. When I use my trouble tree, I am not asking for peace of mind just for myself but also for my family and for my friends and employees too.

Whenever I come to the office, I shake hands with people, most of whom I saw the day before. I act as if we haven't seen each other for days. Even in these days of sexual harassment and political correctness, I want to hug people on my staff. It's just part of my nature. I care very much about the folks I work with. You only get so many chances to express your respect and affection for people, and there's nothing artificial or indifferent about the way I feel about them.

Sometimes I get hit by bad news. It may be bad press, or I may just be feeling down, but when I walk into the office, my employees lift me up. That's the reason I say we are all like family. If I get ripped up in the media, a lot of times I'll get a call from one of my coaches or players or the people on our staff, and they'll say, "George, the people who know you best realize that all that stuff isn't worth the paper it's printed on, so just shake it off. Forget about it. We love you, George. You're our guy and we're behind you."

I think that is so important. The support of friends and family reinforces who you are and what you're all about, and I want to be the kind of person who will do that for other people. When my coach was getting beat up by the media and some of the fans on those bizarre talk shows were giving him a lot of grief, I immediately called him up and told him to forget about it and just keep on doing what he was doing. Professional sports can be a very difficult profession, especially for the coaches. You lose three or four games, and all of a sudden nobody loves you anymore. They're calling for your head.

But my philosophy is simple. Get behind the people you trust, stay with them through thick and thin, and let them know how you feel. That's why I always want my people to know that I'm behind them. That was a lesson I learned from Gary Bettman a couple of years ago. Gary is now commissioner of the National Hockey League, but he was legal counsel for the NBA at that time, and a guy with a level head on his shoulders.

> *Get behind the people you trust, stay with them through thick and thin, and let them know how you feel.*

We had just gone through a difficult period and a highly publicized dispute with our first coach, and I was in the market for a new head coach to lead our team. So I called Gary one day and said, "Gary, can you give me some advice on getting a new coach?"

He said, "Sure, George, I'll be happy to give you some advice. I've given it before and nobody ever listened to me, but I'll give it to you anyway. When you pick somebody, pick whoever you want. I'm not going to suggest that you pick a guy who has been in the pros or college basketball or whatever. You pick the person you want for whatever reasons, but pick somebody you trust and have confidence in. And once you pick him, then stick with him all the way. Don't fire him when he starts losing a few games. Stick with him and give him a chance to develop. What you find is that the teams that have historically won the most games and been the most successful have been the ones that had stability. So pick a good leader and stay with him. That's my advice."

Well, I remembered Gary's advice when I hired Allan Bristow to come in as our new head coach. Even though I got all kinds of criticism about my choice and Allan had to endure a lot of stupid questions, we stuck together and took it one step at a time. One of the biggest advantages of playing basketball in North Carolina is that the fans here are really up on the game. They know what's happening in the league, and they really care about the sport. But that can be a disadvantage sometimes too.

A lot of our fans have followed this game since they were kids, and they know everything about it. They can't turn on the television without seeing the ACC teams or the NBA or some other basketball programs. And these folks can be awfully cruel if they don't like what they see. So we've had to weather some strong winds a time or two.

Many people were critical of the Hornets when we got off to a slow start at the beginning of the 1994–95 season, and our coach was taking a lot of heat. I talked to Allan about the problems, and he suggested I might want to talk to some of the players and get their reactions to what was going on. I thought that was a good idea, so Allan set up the meeting, and, to a man, the players all told me not to worry. Allan is a great coach and things are working fine. They just started slowly, and they were going to pick up the pace in the weeks ahead. "It's a long season," one player told me, "and we'll do fine."

Later, however, some of the Charlotte media heard about my meeting with the team, and a reporter came to ask me some questions. I told him the players said they were happy with the job Coach Bristow is doing and they're confident things are going to pick up very soon. Then the reporter asked me, "Does that mean that if the players had said they wanted a change, Allan would be washing cars somewhere right now?" The reporter smiled, and I thought he was just kidding around, so I laughed, "No, I'd give him a promotion. He'd be flipping hamburgers!"

Well, you can guess what happened then. The next thing I know, the story comes out that George Shinn said Allan Bristow would be flipping hamburgers if the players didn't like the way he was coaching. It may have sounded funny, and it may even have made a good story, but that was neither the spirit nor the intent of what I said. The minute I heard the news, I called Allan and told him what had happened, what was said, and assured him there was no disloyalty in my statement. He was and is the coach of the Hornets, and he has earned not only my respect but that of the players and staff. Allan understood what happened, but it was a while before all the rumors quieted down.

The media's treatment of that story gave the impression that I had gone to the players to check up on my coach, but that was never the case. When Allan set up the meeting with the players, he was simply following basic business strategy and helping me get the input of our frontline people. That's good business, and it worked out great.

Today, the Hornets are playing great basketball, and Allan Bristow is doing a super job as coach. From the start I wanted Allan to know that, win or lose, I was going to be there for him through good times and bad. The media might sting us, the fans might give us a hard time, but we were just going to keep doing things the best way we knew how. We kept at it because I believed we would prove ourselves and come out winners, and I'm happy to say we are seeing the dividends of that philosophy today.

If there is a lesson in all this, it is that you don't get any- where in this world by yourself. I don't care how smart you are or how much money or influence you may have. It takes people working together to achieve success. You don't climb the ladder by yourself. There are always other people not just holding the ladder for you but pushing you up. The thing you must not forget is to reach back and pull those people up with you. You do that because you have faith in yourself and in others.

When you learn to believe, you learn to care for other people and their happiness too. That's part of the system I live by, and it works.

13

When You Don't Get No Respect

ADVERSITY is just a nice word for trouble, and there always seems to be more than enough of it to go around. But trouble doesn't have to control your life; you can learn how to deal with it. When we began hiring people to work for the Charlotte Hornets, I told them, "We have only one goal here, and that's to run a basketball program that makes our fans happy and keeps them coming back." I said, "I know that in the beginning we're not going to win a lot of basketball games. New teams never do. We're going to have a losing team at first, and I've been told that people don't buy tickets to see a losing team. So to stay in business, we've got to do something other than win basketball games to sell tickets."

The object was very simple. "Even if we can't do everything right on the basketball court at first, we can do it right with the food and drinks we serve, with the entertainment and facilities we provide, and with the parking and all the other things that happen off the court. We've got to have better halftime programs than anybody else," I said. "We want to have the best mascot we can have, and everything we do has to be the best we can make it."

Today, I feel that we have done an outstanding job in all those areas, and our fans have rewarded us with their support. But it was a battle in the beginning. I wanted to put a clause in our lease agreement saying that I would have some authority over the hiring of coliseum personnel, but the city said no. Actually, they said, "Shinn, you're crazy! Why would you want to do that?"

I thought it was obvious. I explained, "We're putting on our events in your coliseum, with our team and our fans, and the first contact the fans, our customers, are going to have with our team is your parking-lot attendants. If your guys are rude or discourteous to them or if the fans don't feel they're being treated with respect, they won't come back. That's the reason."

In the old coliseum, some employees would come to work in tank tops and cutoffs, with sweat dripping everywhere, and I said, "We can't afford to have that kind of atmosphere at Hornets games, and if your coliseum managers can't dress their employees properly and in attractive and appropriate uniforms, then we're going to demand the right to decide what they wear." I insisted on that, and I said the lease would be contingent on it. "If you lose money," I said, "I lose money. That's why I want to make sure your people are the best. It's the same way with the ushers. These ushers are going to become family to the season-ticket holders who are here for every game."

The coliseum authority eventually understood my concerns, and even though they wouldn't let me hire the people who worked the Hornets games, they did give us the right to motivate them and to fire them if they didn't perform up to our standards. Those conditions are still included in our lease agreement.

On their side, they stipulated that we would have to supply the uniforms if we wanted to specify the dress code, which was more than acceptable to us. So they published a policy for uniforms and other attire to be worn on duty that has worked out very well. I must also say that the city has been good to me and the Hornets, and I think we've been good for the city as well. It has been a win-win situation for everybody.

Getting It All Together

There were many other matters to be settled, of course, and we often seemed to be going in six directions at once. I had to go back to the architects to make some changes to their plans for the coliseum.

For one thing, the plans called for removing the scoreboard from the old coliseum and hanging it in our brand-new arena. That was a terrible idea. It would have been a colossal embarrassment. They wanted to take an old, out-of-date scoreboard, which is about the size of my desk, and hang it in what was soon to be the largest basketball arena in the entire NBA! So after I had looked into the options, we ordered the current scoreboard and had it designed and built specifically for our facility.

It's a monster! Actually, it's an eight-sided beauty, with a video screen on four of the eight sides and complete digital scoreboard information on the other four sides. During the game there are all kinds of exciting graphic effects, visual explosions, *Zap!* messages, scoring stats, and other images of that sort. We also sell commercial messages that are creative and fun and popular with the crowds.

We agreed to put up the money to buy the new scoreboard and donate it to the city. Proceeds from the sale of advertising were to be used to pay off the cost of the board, then once

167

it was paid for, the Hornets were to split any additional proceeds with the city.

That was another no-lose situation for Charlotte. While we were at it, I also put up the money for terrazzo floors, special signs and equipment, color coding, and skyboxes. We decided to sell the skyboxes to individuals and organizations and to pay for their completion with the proceeds. All those things have been extremely successful, and the fans have responded enthusiastically. In fact, the only team that has ever outsold us in novelty sales was the Chicago Bulls when they were the league champions. We surpassed the Bulls in the 1993–94 season.

In the beginning, as I indicated earlier, we were not selling out every game, so we decided to put more money into the marketing effort. We spent more money on halftime programs than any other team. Before long the fans started coming, and we not only sold out every game, but we sold the maximum number of season tickets available. Our very first year in the league, we were an incredible success. We led the league in attendance.

> *The only team that has ever outsold us in novelty sales was the Chicago Bulls when they were the league champions.*

Our goal was to make Hornets basketball an event for everyone, so people could feel that they had fun, saw a great game, were royally entertained, had good food and drinks, and got their money's worth in every way. I think that's one of the main reasons we lead the league in attendance.

Of course, we also lead the league in spending the most money for halftime shows, pre- and post-game activities, and all the other perks our fans enjoy. Some people ask me, "Why do you do that, George? You don't need to. You've got them lined up to buy tickets as it is. They're paying you $100 a head to be on a waiting list!"

"Well, that's one of the reasons we get them," I say, "because we care about those things." We want basketball to be

168

fun and exciting—the main part of a total entertainment experience. We are saying to our fans, "We love you and we appreciate your support." And they know that.

If you go to a game at the Boston Gardens and if you don't happen to be a real basketball nut, chances are you are going to be very disappointed. They have one guy up in the loft who plays an organ—I wouldn't allow an organ in our arena—but other than that, they do virtually nothing for their fans. I have never heard of their having any type of halftime activity. They don't have a mascot. They just set their sights on having great players and winning. If you are a pure basketball enthusiast, that may be enough for you, but there's just not much there for the general spectator who wants to be entertained and have some fun.

Total Entertainment

Today, we do a lot of things with and for our fans. We involve them in the life of the team and in many special events.

We have rented the entire Paramount Carowinds Theme Park for our season-ticket holders. It's like Six Flags. Not as big as Walt Disney World perhaps, but it's our big theme park, and all our season-ticket holders were invited to come and ride the rides and enjoy all the shows and amusements as our guests. We brought in some of the great musical groups from the fifties and sixties, like the Four Tops and the Temptations, and we also had some younger pop and rock 'n' roll entertainers.

The players came out to the theme park to meet the fans. They posed for pictures with them, signed autographs, and got to know our supporters one-on-one. Obviously, to rent that whole theme park and let the fans come in free of charge cost us a lot of money. It would be more than we could pay for in any one or two games, but we did it because, first of all, we like our fans and enjoy their company and, second, because we want to show them that we really care. Many of our sponsors and key people have participated in these events, and we try to have some kind of fan-team activities taking place continuously.

The design of our season tickets is one more indication of the attention to detail we like to put into things. I suppose most of our season-ticket holders don't even realize how unique it is, but if they were in another city they would probably get a cheap little book of tickets—a standardized packet that is just run through a computer and stapled together. Our season tickets have beautiful color photos on them, featuring great moments in Hornets basketball history, game-winning shots, super slam dunks or blocked shots, as well as action shots of our players. We do that for all forty-one home games.

> *Our season tickets have beautiful color photos on them, featuring great moments in Hornets basketball history.*

Now, obviously that costs money, but it's just one more advantage for our fans. Things like that make the Hornets unique, and it really contributes to our incredible fan loyalty. We realize, of course, that there's only a small handful of our season-ticket holders who are able to attend every single game. We know that. And if all they had was one of those cheap little ticket books, they probably wouldn't pull out all their old tickets. But if it has a nice picture on it, their kids or grandkids are going to want the tickets, so they go ahead and pull the tickets out to give to friends or relatives, or to keep as souvenirs.

A lot of our fans get them, keep them, and have them framed. Every year we see some beautiful collections. I have a huge frame in my office with all those pictures in them. We also keep complete sets that we can give to special friends of the Hornets and to our sponsors. This is one way we can say thank you to the people who have supported the Hornets— we can give them a piece of our history.

One of the fringe benefits of this is that when the season is over and our fans look in their ticket books and see that all their tickets are gone, they know it's time to renew. If they missed half of the games and all they had were the cheap little computer tickets, they might decide they had wasted their money. "Look at this," they'd say, "I still have twenty unused tickets. Maybe I don't need to renew my season ticket for next year."

With our tickets, however, most of the time they have already ripped out all those tickets, so they don't even think about the games they may have missed. They remember the ones they attended, they remember all those beautiful pictures, and they remember all the good times they had, and when they see their empty ticket book, they don't hesitate to renew their season tickets. It's a simple concept, but there is a psychological component to it, and we think that works to our advantage. Plus, it's a little something extra for our fans that they won't get anywhere else.

To the Next Level
The Hornets raise in excess of half a million dollars for charity every year through the efforts of our team projects and a golf tournament. We also sponsor a fund-raiser called "Top Hats and High Tops," which is very popular with our fans. From the waist up the players are supposed to dress in formal attire: bow tie, pleated shirt, cummerbund, the works. That's the "top hat" part. But from the waist down, they wear shorts and sneakers—that's the "high tops" part. Our friends and fans bid for tables based on which players are seated there. We auction off memorabilia signed by the players, Hornets sneakers, basketballs, and many other things. The money that is raised goes to a variety of different charities, including the Special Olympics, Children's Hospital here in Charlotte, and others. In our first six years, we have generated more than $3 million through our various team charities and other programs supported by the Shinn Foundation.

We get the players involved in all these events. Instead of me or the coaches and staff dictating which charities we should support, the whole team takes part, because without the personal involvement of our players, it wouldn't be successful. We let them help determine the best causes and the type of fund-raising activities to be involved with. When they are involved in it, the players are going to be more energetic, and it is always more fun for everybody that way. We require that our players give a certain amount of their time to these events, but they do it willingly in most cases because they believe in what we're doing.

You have to realize that, as talented as they are, the players are still very young, and they enjoy having a good time and doing all the things young people do. But I want to be an example to my players and encourage them to see that their success and their personal wealth give them responsibilities to the community. On some teams, the players seem to go wild. They take everything they can get and give nothing back. That won't work here. Being an adult means that you have to take responsibility for yourself and that you try to be an example for the fans who are watching you. There are so many people who look up to the players, and I feel strongly that they need to appreciate their own leadership responsibilities and realize that they are role models to many young people. Sometimes I feel as if I am a sort of surrogate parent to some of our guys, but it's a role I enjoy. That's part of my job.

I try to extend the same courtesy to the players that they have shown me. When Muggsy Bogues's father died, for example, we chartered a private plane and flew some of our players, coaches, and team personnel up for the funeral. And when Dell Curry's father died, we did the same thing. I think it is important for me to be there. We are more than just a team; we're a family. When new players come into our organization, I try to let them know that we are family, and that's the approach we take on and off the court.

Even with thousands of screaming fans and with all the celebrity that surrounds this business, it can be lonely out there unless you have a support group that cares for you and stands by you in the tough times. So that's why we do it, and that's why we become like family to each other.

Community Relations

I try to make the point that our team and players are part of our city and that we care about the welfare of our community as much as anyone else. Sometimes, in certain situations, we may have the resources to help in an exceptional way. That happened not long ago when two Charlotte police officers were killed in an inner-city neighborhood. Due to the racial problems and media involvement, it became a volatile situation and there was a lot of name-calling. When I saw what was happening, I wanted to help both sides.

My first concern was for the families of the two police officers, of course. They had suffered a tragic loss and needed help and compassion, so we offered to provide the transportation for one of the families to fly back to their home, about two hundred miles away. Then, later, as a tribute to these two valiant men and as a commitment to the community, we offered to pay the salaries for two extra police officers on the Charlotte police department. We paid two salaries outside the city budget in honor of those officers who fell in the line of duty, and we continue that program to this day.

Then I wanted to show support for the people in the inner city and help to relieve some of the frustrations they were feeling. I thought, what better way for a basketball team to show concern than to help refurbish the basketball courts in some of those tough neighborhoods where kids needed a place to play? So we set up a program to refurbish or rebuild several courts. We required the local people who would be using the facilities to put some sweat equity into it themselves by helping build them. They were asked to paint stripes and help clean up the grounds, and they were to keep it up. Also, to assure that the people in the neighborhood would feel a rightful sense of ownership, we asked them to raise part of the

173

money, not for their basketball court, but as seed money for building basketball courts in other housing projects.

A lot of times basketball courts in inner-city neighborhoods take a lot of abuse, and within days even the best of them can get pretty well torn up. But we made sure the kids in these neighborhoods felt it was their court. They helped build it, and they had pride in it. When we celebrated the one-year anniversary for that first court, not only was it still in great shape but the nets were still up. And as a sign of community reconciliation, the court was named in honor of one of the officers who had been killed there.

I think it is so important that we not give up on the human spirit and that we hang on to our faith in people. People don't need handouts. Instead, they need to be involved and to have a sense of purpose and pride. I say, give people an opportunity and they will take pride in it. Building those basketball courts was just one example. We extended a hand and the people showed their support. And the fact that those nets were still up a year later, as small as that may seem, was an indication to me of the people's willingness to improve their circumstances.

> *People don't need handouts. They need to be involved and to have a sense of purpose and pride.*

The Changing Scene

Even after we got the franchise, there were still plenty of naysayers in Charlotte who were saying the team would flop. When we started selling bunches of season tickets, they predicted it was just a matter of time until we went belly-up. Bones McKinney, who was one of the top NCAA coaches at Wake Forest University, had been very critical of me and my plans for the Hornets before we ever landed the franchise. Every time the media approached him, he would blast us and our ideas and offer prophecies of doom for the citizens of Charlotte.

At one point the press went to McKinney and asked if his opinion of the Hornets had changed in light of our success. You would naturally expect the guy to look at our attendance, our win-loss record, and our incredible fan loyalty, and say, "Well, I guess I made a mistake. They've done quite a job." But no. He said the honeymoon would be over next year. He predicted that next year we'd find out what it's like to hit bottom. And there were many others, including some of the old guard, who fought us tooth and nail. Actually I get a feeling of satisfaction knowing that the street in front of the Charlotte Coliseum is named for one of our most vocal critics. It is a constant reminder of the way things can change.

It has been interesting to see just how much things have changed over the past few years. Before the team arrived in town and before we played our first game, I was constantly in the newspapers. Regardless of what the Hornets did, rather than Larry Johnson's or Alonzo Mourning's picture, it was mine plastered all over the papers. But, fortunately, once we started playing our first regular season, I was quickly moved to the background, and the players and coaches became the big news.

But when your face isn't seen in print all that often, people don't recognize you so easily. They may know your name, but they can't always put the name with the face. I found that out one embarrassing night.

I had been invited to speak at a civic club in Gastonia, North Carolina, which is not far from Charlotte. My secretary had typed up the directions for me, but I thought I could find the place, so I didn't pay much attention to them. I sure found out why they call it the "country" club, because it was really out in the country, and I had a lot of trouble finding it. To say I got lost would be an understatement. I got lost, big time, and I was afraid I was going to miss my speech.

I kept driving around, trying to find the road, and I couldn't. I realized that either I had to get back to the main road and follow the directions or I needed to stop and get some help. I only had ten minutes to get there. However, I

175

was sensitive about stopping at just any store, because my face had been in all the newspapers and I didn't want to admit to everybody in Gastonia that I was lost.

I started looking for a store that wasn't very populated. I drove right by a couple of service stations where men were standing outside shooting the breeze. I wasn't about to stop there.

But then I noticed a little convenience store with only one car in the drive. I pulled up to the front door, threw open the car door, left the engine running, and ran inside. There was a middle-aged lady at the counter, and I said, "Ma'am, I am lost. I need directions to Gastonia Country Club. Can you help me?"

She looked at me and got a big smile on her face, and she said, "I know who you are."

"You do?" I said nervously.

"Yes, I do," she said. "You're Muggsy Bogues!"

When I got to the country club (with the help of that lady's good directions), I told them that story. I guess they must have laughed for ten solid minutes. And after the speech, as I went to sit down, all anybody wanted to know was, "Where was that store?"

14

Working with People

AT one point, too many people had their own agendas for the Charlotte Hornets, and I had to make sure that they understood that I would be the one to lay out the course for this team. Early on we went through some hard times with coaches and players, and that's the reason there were some highly publicized firings and staff changes. Perhaps there is no better example of this than the battle with our former coach, Dick Harter.

What caused me the most problems was that he tried to create dissension between me and the rest of the staff. He took a dislike to Muggsy Bogues, and he made up his mind that, one way or the other, he was going to get Muggsy out of there. If he couldn't trade him, he wanted to just toss him off the team at any cost. That was a big mistake, for many reasons.

One day in our second season, Dick came storming into my office, demanding to see me. We had a very unpleasant exchange, during which he told me that I knew nothing about basketball and that we were never going to make a go of this thing unless we traded several of our key players. His arrogance and profanity convinced me that it was the coach who had to go, not the players.

Well, the meeting didn't end much better than it started. I met with our executives, told them what had happened, and we discussed the pros and cons of keeping Harter around. It would be expensive to let him go, but it was clear he was more of a liability than an asset to the Hornets. I thought, *If a guy would behave that way with me, knowing that I own the team and have $30 million invested in it, I can't even imagine how he must be treating everyone else. If he treats me like a child, belittles me, and tells me I'm hopelessly ignorant, then what is he saying to my players and the rest of the staff?*

Controversial Decisions

I expected there to be repercussions from the decision to fire Harter—that kind of news always makes headlines. Unfortunately, the actual circumstances surrounding the eventual dismissal of Dick Harter turned out to be even more difficult than they had to be. I had arranged with Carl Scheer, who was our general manager at the time, to give him the word that night in San Antonio, where we were going to be playing. Carl said, "I'll go down to Texas, George, but I'd like you to go with me when I give him the news."

For some reason, though, Carl decided to call Dick on the phone before we left Charlotte, and he fired him over the phone. Predictably, Dick was angry and upset, and he immediately called a press conference with all the local media and the beat reporters who follow the team and told them he had been fired for trying to do his job.

As you can imagine, that news went off like a canon, and the photographers and reporters were waiting for me when I got to the Charlotte Airport. That was the first I knew that Carl Scheer had already fired Dick by telephone. When I walked into the airport terminal, the cameras were everywhere. There were microphones and TV lights in my face. "Why did you fire Dick Harter?" they demanded.

"I didn't fire Dick Harter," I said. That wasn't supposed to happen until later that evening in San Antonio. I wondered how they had gotten the word ahead of time.

Several reporters yelled at me, "We just spoke with Harter, and he said that Carl Scheer called him today and told him he was fired. We understand that you are on your way to San Antonio now to make it official."

> *I wondered how they had gotten the word ahead of time.*

I said, "Well, we'll make that announcement when it is done."

Just as I was trying to defuse the situation and get to my plane the next bombshell hit. "Did you know that Dick's brother died today?"

"What?" I asked.

"Dick's brother had been sick for a long time, and he just died today. Right after Dick got the bad news from his family, he found out you were going to fire him. Why did you pick this day, of all days, to fire your coach?"

Of course I had no idea anything like that had happened; I didn't even know Dick had a brother.

"Well, it seems a little odd that you would fire a man on the same day that he found out his brother had died."

The timing was obviously bad, and Carl had made a mistake by calling Harter on the telephone and telling him the news ahead of time. When I called home later that evening,

Carolyn told me, "The news media is butchering you, George. They're making you look pretty bad."

"What's new?" I said.

Losing the Players

It should have been obvious to anyone who thought about it that I was not firing Dick because his brother died. I didn't need to take advantage of the man's weakness to let him go. I was firing him because he was a bad coach and had lost the respect of his players.

I remember making the statement to the media, "Look, obviously the timing was bad, but you have to understand that we had to do what we did. Maybe you don't agree with our decision right now, but you will, because we made the right decision for this team. And I don't apologize for that. We had to do it."

Later, Harter turned around and sued us even though we had already agreed to pay him everything he had been promised in his contract. In his deposition, he made the statement, "George Shinn is dumb to think that he knows anything about basketball! He honestly believes that Dell Curry and Muggsy Bogues can play basketball." By saying that, he shot himself in the foot.

If anyone was using poor judgment, it was a coach who would make that kind of statement in a deposition. His words were arrogant, disrespectful, and insulting, besides being wrong. For one thing, Dell Curry received the Sixth Man Award for the 1993–1994 season. Coming off the bench, he is arguably the best player in the entire NBA. Muggsy Bogues leads the league in several categories as point guard, and he was voted Most Valuable Player (MVP) by Hornets fans that same year. All this is in light of the fact that Alonzo Mourning and Larry Johnson were the biggest superstars on the team.

Alonzo and Larry have a lot of respect and affection for Muggsy Bogues, and they loved it when he was picked as MVP. Muggsy has an incredible fast break, and he is sixth in the NBA in number of assists per game. But most of all, Muggsy plays with heart, and the big guys respect that. Everyone knows that smaller players like Muggsy bring another dimension and a higher level of excitement to the game. Muggsy does that for us. He has a way of making everybody play better because he's got such heart.

Dick Harter was an excellent X-and-O guy as a coach. He was a strategist, a defensive expert, and a true analyst of the game. But he wasn't the right coach for the Hornets, and the parting of the ways was inevitable. Needless to say, we won the lawsuit.

Too Hot to Handle

Muggsy has been the heart of the team for a long time, and he's a great illustration of my own story. Here's a guy who is just five-foot-three, but through talent, discipline, and sheer determination, he has made it in a world of giants, where the average height is six-foot-eight. Think about it! It's absolutely astonishing to realize that a young man who is nearly two feet shorter than the average player in the league can keep up with the best of them, and create a spirit of fun and excitement at the same time.

Muggsy is a great example of what's right with the NBA.

I remember that Coach Dean Smith used to tell his players at the University of North Carolina, "When you go up against Muggsy, if you don't see him, just make sure you keep the ball as high as you can. If you try to hold the ball at waist height, that little fox will come in and jerk it out of your hands. Hold it low and he's got it, so keep that ball up!" And he was absolutely right.

Muggsy will go between a taller player's legs to get the ball. We have pictures of him doing it, dribbling the ball right past the biggest athletes on the court. He is incredible. In the fast break, he can get it moving faster than anyone I have ever seen. He can dish it out just like the bigger players. Nobody should ever sell Muggsy short.

I use Muggsy as an example quite often when I'm talking to kids. They can identify with Muggsy. He's shorter than the other players, he is trying to compete with guys who are twice as big as he is, and yet he works hard and helps us win basketball games. Muggsy is a great example of what's right with the NBA, and he makes life easier for all of us. He also knows that if he ever has a problem, he can call me and I will be there.

It's not always so simple. Sometimes we come across players who need constant attention. They have behavior, morale, or moral problems, and it is very hard to work with people like that or to keep them productive.

One of the most widely publicized players we ever recruited was J. R. Reed, who was a great basketball player and one of the most natural talents I've ever seen. He was born and raised just north of us in Virginia, and he was a superstar at the University of North Carolina. People were saying he was the best player ever to come out of the South. The great Julius Irving once said that if he were starting a new NBA team and could pick anybody in the league, he would pick J. R. Reed, and that was when Reed was still a freshman in college.

We picked him as a junior, when he came out early, but he didn't materialize for us. And there were other problems. How do you talk to a twenty-two-year-old multimillionaire who needs to get his act together? Roger Schweickert, our vice president who works with these kinds of problems, has had to face that challenge many times. Over the years we have found that when a player is too hot to handle, the best solution is often to give him some room, and a chance to play somewhere else.

I much prefer to work things out one-on-one. For example, Rex Chapman was our first ever draft pick, in the 1988 season. As with a lot of first-round picks, there was a lot of bargaining on the contract, and at some point we reached a stalemate. So I asked Rex and his father to come over to my house to talk in a more informal atmosphere. Spencer Stolpen and I sat down and talked with the Chapmans and their agent, David Falk. We had some cookies and punch and got to know each other's concerns.

After a while, Rex and I went for a walk, and I said to him, "Rex, we picked you first because we want you here. We think you're our kind of player. You have talent, a good attitude, and we think you would be an important part of our club." He told me his concerns and hopes, and I assured him we could work through all those things. When we got back to the house, Rex said he was ready to sign and he wanted to be a Charlotte Hornet.

Calming the Doubters

I believe that if you do things the right way and for the right reasons, good things will happen. I use the example that in two consecutive lotteries, we got the top draft picks: Larry Johnson and Alonzo Mourning. Larry was a holdout also, but we finally signed him. There was a lot of jockeying, and some of that got into the media. As a result Larry took a lot of abuse. The fans tend to hold it against a player who holds out. Once he signs, it's the team's responsibility to get him back into the good graces of our supporters. At that point, he is part of the team and we all have to work together.

Larry wanted to be more than just another player. Charlotte was his adopted home, and he cared about the city, so he found a beautiful way of showing how he felt. It turned out that the United Way, which almost never misses its fundraising goals, came up $180,000 short that year, and word went out that they weren't going to be able to keep their commitments. So Larry called them and said he wanted to help out. He wrote the United Way a personal check for the entire amount. Needless to say, the fans came around quickly, and at the next game they gave LJ a standing ovation. Later, he was invited to the White House to meet the president, who personally thanked him for his generous gift to the United Way. That was the first time any professional athlete had made such a generous donation.

A year later, Larry signed an extension with us for $84

million, the largest contract ever signed by a professional athlete. Again, sports pages all over the country were filled with stories about the big contract. But there's a lot more to this game than money and shooting hoops. All these players can play good basketball at this level. I maintain that the difference between the good players and the great ones is character, and we spend a lot of time and resources checking on the character of our players before we sign them.

A few years ago an owner who is no longer in the league called and asked me about an ACC player who was in the draft that year, and he wanted to know how I rated him. Ironically, the player was Joe Wolf, who plays for us now, and he is a great guy. I said I thought he was a good player, good height, not terribly fast, but had a good jump shot, and most important, he was a good kid. I said, "He has good character, and he'd be an asset to your club." At that point the other owner exploded. "Are you nuts, Shinn? Let me tell you something. You don't build a basketball club by looking for guys that are nice boys. You've got to find good ballplayers and put that other crap behind you."

I said to myself, *How wrong can somebody be?* For me, it's not just a theory but a management strategy. It's based on the conviction that the difference between a good player and a great one is character.

Worth the Effort?

When I think about some of the unfortunate experiences we have had with a few players, I realize it would have been too costly and too much work to keep them around. I have always talked to our coaches about it, and many times we find we have no option but to trade for players who will be more compatible with our system. I try to do the best I can to make sure we pick players who are not just talented athletes but also disciplined people. It's enough of a challenge working with players who are young, rich, and aggressive, but if they've got bad habits or a record of drugs and wild parties, it is better to let them play somewhere else. Sooner or later, players who can't control themselves off the court are going to cause you trouble both on and off the court.

I've tried counseling some of the players when it looks like they are losing their focus on the game and getting into other things. I say, "Look, man, you've got a great career ahead of you. Why do you want to mess it up? Can't you just get your act together and play basketball?" While talk doesn't always help, we're pleased to have had our share of success stories.

> **"Do you think we could do something to help him get turned around and back on the right track?"**

David Wingate, who is one of the most versatile players in the league, had some charges against him while he was playing for San Antonio, and there was some question about whether or not he could stay in the league. Most of the charges were dropped or settled out of court, and when he became a free agent, his agent contacted us, and our coaches came to talk to me about it. They knew that, based on David's history of off-court problems, I was going to be very leery of signing him, but they still wanted to talk.

I sat down with Dave Twardzik, who is our director of player personnel, and he told me, "Here are the facts on the kid, George. Do we pursue him or not?"

I looked over the whole file, stats, press clips, charges, and I said, "No, we don't."

Allan Bristow, our coach, said, "Can we just turn our backs on this kid, George? Here's a talented player who can help this club. We can't find anybody better, and we need somebody now. Do you think we could do something to help him get turned around and back on the right track? Could we talk to him and tell him about our concerns and say that we're willing to give him an opportunity to play ball again?"

Well, that rang a bell with me, so I said, "OK, I like the idea of extending a helping hand. You can try it, Allan, if you think it's the right thing to do."

So I gave Dave Twardzik and Spencer Stolpen the OK to

185

look him over, and I said, "If you can talk to David's agent and tell him the type of club we have here and if he will come to terms with us, then you have my blessing to give him a try. We have a family here, and we believe in doing things in a positive way. We believe in community involvement, we believe in doing good things for people, and we won't put up with anything that will take away from that. But tell him we are also forgiving if he wants to play basketball."

I told them that there had to be one clear understanding. "If he gets even one charge against him—it does not have to be a conviction, just any noise at all—he's out of here, and we don't have to guarantee the contract." I said, "If he'll sign a contract with those stipulations, knowing that we are going to police him as well as try to help him succeed here, then I'm willing to try him. But, gentlemen," I added, "if anything happens, he's history." They put all that in the contract. Wingate signed, we signed, and today we're glad we did.

Before long, though, there was an article in the paper. One of the sportswriters said, "Well, the squeaky-clean image of the Hornets has vanished." It was a cheap shot. They wrote about all the problems that Wingate has had, and they didn't give us a pat on the back for giving the guy a chance. The way they put it, he was going to be on parole while he was here. "If Wingate gets out of line," they said, "bam, he's back in jail." But it was never really that austere. He is a little older and wiser now, and we think some of our other players have been a good influence. He hasn't been in trouble since he's been with the Hornets, and that's been more than two years.

The coaches were right. Dave Wingate has been a big asset to our club. He is one of the best, if not *the* best defensive player we have. When he comes off the bench, he is one of the best in the NBA, and I like the fact that he played on the same team with Muggsy in high school in Baltimore, Dunbar. Reggie Lewis, who played at Boston, was also on that team. All five starters from that school made it to the pros. Muggsy Bogues was the long shot of the group, and obviously he has made NBA history in Charlotte.

15

Being Faithful Means Being There

BEING there for our players is important. Whether it means showing faith and confidence in them, giving them a second chance, or sometimes being a sort of parent to some of them, the effort of keeping an organization like ours running, and keeping people productive, calls for loyalty, flexibility, and courage. We have tried to make the Charlotte Hornets a club with a sense of personal commitment, but even when you have all those things down pat and even when you work closely with people, the past can still come back to haunt you sometimes.

Spencer Stolpen is one of the most talented and capable

men I have ever met. He was hired to work in one of our schools in Fort Lauderdale. He had a law degree from Syracuse University. I didn't understand why he would want to teach in our little business college, but we were glad to have him. It was clear from the start that he was an able and talented instructor.

Over a period of time, Spencer showed himself to be very capable, and when the position opened, we hired him as president of the college. At the time the hiring request came through proposing that we move him into that position, I asked the local manager, "How do you get a guy with a law degree from Syracuse University, and a lawyer at that, to be president of a small four-year college?" We didn't usually get people with credentials like that working for the money we paid, but the manager didn't have an answer either.

As we continued to grow, we had to make other changes in the organization. At one point we needed to find a legal adviser to work with us. I had met Spencer by that time, and I was impressed with him. He was bright, energetic, and seemed committed to the business-school program and what we were trying to do. I had learned that he and his family are observant Jews, which means that they are serious about their faith and attend synagogue, but that did not affect my judgment one way or the other. Spencer was very talented and capable, and the fact that he happened to be of a different religion did not concern me.

If I had any concern at all about his religious beliefs, it probably had more to do with how other Protestants who knew how seriously I take my own faith might react when they heard that I had hired someone who happened to be of the Jewish faith as president of our business college in Fort Lauderdale. Other than that, I never gave it a second thought. The one question that did keep coming back to me, though, was how was it that we were able to hire a man with Spencer's qualifications to come to work for us at that little college in Fort Lauderdale?

A Good Legal Mind

During that time we had been spending a lot of money on legal fees. We had schools all over the country, and there were constant legal questions, issues that called for skilled legal judgment, contract negotiations, protection of our franchise rights and business identity, and so on. From a business standpoint, legal retainers and court fees are high-cost items, so when I began looking for ways to cut costs and improve profitability, one issue was perfectly clear: We needed to reduce our legal expenses.

At one point our legal expenses and attorneys' fees were much too high. I mentioned to one of our executives that if we had somebody in-house who could help us take care of that situation, counsel with us on important business decisions, and help us to come up with legal positions on all those critical issues, then we could improve our financial and legal situation at the same time. If we had legal problems in another city and needed to coordinate with attorneys in those places, or simply correspond with the civil justice system in another jurisdiction, then it

> *His insight into the school business was one of the key factors in my decision to simplify my life and sell the schools.*

would be good to have someone who could make sure we got the best people, the best prices, and the best legal advice available. Having someone like that on staff could save us a lot of money, so we began looking for someone to serve as full-time counsel.

The people who were running the schools at that time recommended Spencer for the job. They said that he was already familiar with our organization and had been working in it for several years. He had a law degree and had been licensed as an attorney, so the choice seemed simple. I said, "That's fine. If you all agree that Spencer is the man for the job, then offer him the position." The salary we offered wasn't an enormous amount of money, but we offered him the job and he took it.

Within a matter of weeks, Spencer became very important to me in making critical business decisions. His insight into the school business was one of the key factors in my decision to simplify my life and sell the schools. Spencer helped prepare the offering and arrange all the legal documents, and the sale went through with very few glitches. I remember reading somewhere that now and then every good business needs a tough guy, and when we needed him to make hard decisions, Spencer could fill that bill as well as anybody.

He's tough and he can say no in a minute. Nobody would ever call Spencer Stolpen a yes-man. I believe that can even be seen in the way he handled my stroke. A yes-man would have said, "Yes sir, Mr. Shinn," when I was telling everybody to leave me alone. A yes-man would have just let me die. But Spencer knew something was wrong, and he decided to do something about it. He would not let me refuse the help I needed.

He's not just tough; he is also brilliant, and I have gained a lot of respect and admiration for this man over the years that we have worked together. He now serves as president of the Hornets, and we've weathered many storms together.

The Roots of Bitterness

As I've already mentioned, we ran into difficulties with a couple of the partners in the original Hornets ownership group when I wanted to buy them out. Rick Hendrick acknowledged my right to buy out his interest without hesitation. Cy Bahakel and Felix Sabates, on the other hand, resisted, and rather than just sign off and accept a negotiated settlement, they decided to ignore the signed agreement and reject my purchase offer.

Felix began looking for ways to stop the purchase. Rick told me that Felix was going around telling people that Spencer was a disbarred lawyer, and he said I could expect to see the whole thing in the papers before long. The next thing we knew, the story hit the front page of the *Charlotte Observer*, saying that George Shinn's right-hand man, the president of the Charlotte Hornets, was a disbarred lawyer who had dealings with underworld figures in Florida.

I was shocked and angry when I saw that story—not at Spencer—at whoever planted the story. I had never suspected anyone in our organization of taking part in illegal activities. I asked Spencer to come over to my office and tell me what was going on. I said, "Spencer, I don't know what's going on or what this is all about, but I have never asked you about your past, and you never had any reason to tell me about it. Should I have asked?

"The only suspicion I ever had," I added, "was wondering how we could afford such a highly qualified lawyer like you to come to work for us in our business schools, especially when the salary we could pay you at that time was not very large. I suppose that didn't exactly add up, but we were glad to have you. Spencer, is there something I need to know about? Is there something I might have missed?" I could see that he was a little nervous about all this, so I said, "Why don't you just tell me the story?"

Spencer said, "George, when I graduated from law school, I was like most young attorneys. I wanted to be a lawyer and start my own practice. Just as I was trying to find a place to get started in the profession, a situation opened up that seemed like a golden opportunity for me. A man who was known to have some rough connections in Florida offered me a job. It included a nice office, a place to hang out my shingle, and on top of that, he was going to pay me an annual retainer in excess of $40,000 a year. That was a lot of money for a young lawyer in those days, and he said I wouldn't have to do anything illegal to get it. All he asked was that I help him stay out of trouble. I'm not saying I approved of everything he was doing, but I believed every citizen is entitled to legal protection, so I took the job."

Spencer told me more details of his employment, and then

191

he said that at one point somebody died under suspicious circumstances and the police had eventually traced it back to this big operator and his organization. It was all over the news for a few weeks, and apparently Spencer's name and photo appeared on TV a time or two. So here is Spencer in a very difficult situation. He is married with two young children. He had allowed his employer to deposit a large sum of money in his checking account, and at some point funds were apparently transferred illegally. Spencer said, "I don't know if the money was laundered or what the deal was, but it was going through my account, and all of a sudden things were looking pretty bad for me.

"When the big operator was arrested," he told me, "the district attorney subpoenaed all my records. And what went through my mind at that instant was that I had a wife and two kids. How could I protect them? I was caught between two terrible alternatives. If I failed to turn over my records, chances are I would be disbarred and I might even go to jail. But if I did turn them over, then my employer was going to jail for sure, and harm could come to me or my family.

"As you might guess," he said, "I was terrified. I decided I only had one choice in that situation—I burned all my files. I did it knowing that I would probably lose my license and my law practice, but at least I wouldn't jeopardize my family's well-being, and I would have a chance to start a new life.

"George," Spencer said, "there are many things I might have done differently. That was the choice I felt I had to make at that time. And if I had to make the same choice again, I would probably do the same thing. I couldn't afford to turn that man in. Above everything else I was determined to protect my family."

192

I said, "Spencer, you don't have to explain anything else to me. I understand. I'm very sorry somebody felt he had to bring all this out in the open right now. But it happened, and I guess it's going to be on both our shoulders for a while, so let's just try to get through this thing and hold on for the ride."

Spencer said, "Are you going to fire me?"

"Fire you!" I said, "Goodness, no, Spencer, I'm not going to fire you! You have been loyal to me. You have been very supportive. You have been a good friend and a tremendous employee, and even if it turns out that the general public can't forgive you, you can be sure that God can forgive you, and I want you to know that I can forgive you too. Let's just go forward and try to rise above all this. It may come back to haunt us for years to come, but if you keep doing the good job you have always done for me all these years, people are going to forget about the bad stuff and respect you for what you're doing."

And so Spencer and I just kept on going until things eventually came back to normal. He has been loyal to me from the first, and he has always tried to do what was best both for me and the Hornets. I have immense respect for the man. Today, Spencer is one of the most capable executives in the NBA, and that's not my opinion alone. Many people would agree with me.

> *"Even if it turns out that the general public can't forgive you, you can be sure that God can forgive you, and I can forgive you, too."*

Along the way I have learned a lot about his depth of faith, and it has crossed my mind more than once that Spencer is more honest, considerate, compassionate, and caring than many people I know who claim to be Christians. He doesn't curse or fly off the handle, no matter how upset he gets. He just won't do it, and I admire a guy who has that kind of self-control. I have never seen him smoke a cigarette or drink alcohol or take the Lord's name in vain. Unfortunately, I can't say that for a lot of other people.

Being Faithful at Home

Through these kinds of experiences I have learned a lot about other people, and I have had to carry some of those lessons home with me a time or two. Carolyn and I have three children, two boys and a girl. The oldest is our son Chris, who is a musician on the West Coast. The middle child is our daughter, Susan, who is interested in cheerleading at the moment. And Chad, our youngest, is a budding athlete. Each of our children is unique, and they all have their own interests. They are great kids and they give us a lot of pleasure, but we worry sometimes. Let me explain.

At one time I tried very hard to get my oldest son to take an interest in sports. The first time I saw the announcement on the bulletin board at his school saying we could sign up for T-ball, I was one of the first parents in line. I did everything I could to get Chris interested in sports. I offered to help him physically. I told him about all the motivational principles I had learned from sports. I said that athletics would teach him the value of winning, losing, and honest competition. I even told him that sports is a great way for young people to make new friends, and I suggested it would be a tremendous asset for him as he was growing up. I felt that athletics was one of the only things that kept me on the straight and narrow when I was a kid, so I really pushed the idea.

I did everything I could to sell Chris on it. I had a batting cage installed in our backyard, along with a professional pitching machine. I mean, I did it all! At one time we had a tennis court in the backyard that we hardly ever used, so I had it converted into a basketball court with regulation-size NBA goals at each end, and the floors were painted with the Hornets' colors. I even put in a powerful outdoor-lighting system so the kids could practice at night. But Chris never got into it.

Part of the reason, no doubt, was that he was not interested in athletics. He didn't have the desire to be a starter on any of his teams. Today, he tells me the only reason he continued with sports in school was because he knew how much it meant to me—which shows the love and respect he had for me. But sometimes you have to let your children go the way their hearts are leading them instead of trying to lead them in a direction that you would prefer for them to go. I'm not saying I learned this all at once, but I came to see that it's their life, and even the most concerned parent has to back off at some point and let the kids live it their own way.

I learned a lesson from all this, and by the time our youngest son was old enough to take part in organized sports, I realized that I needed to encourage him a little less enthusiastically—to simply make sure he had the opportunity to play. I wanted him to find out for himself if he liked sports. It must have worked, because today he participates in all sports, and he just loves it. He seems to feel about them a lot like the way I did when I was his age.

In his first year in T-ball, when Chad was just six, there were thirteen home runs hit in the whole league—and Chad hit eleven of them. He started off as a star in sports, and nearly every year he made all-star on the baseball team. T-ball is like Little League baseball. In the beginning, before the kids are able to hit a pitched ball, they hit the ball off a big tee. Later, they move up to a pitching machine, or the coach pitches for them, and then finally they move on to regular pitchers. In his last year in junior high, Chad was the leading hitter in the Babe Ruth League. He had the most extra-base hits, and he was the leading scorer on his junior high basketball team at the same time.

> *There were thirteen home runs hit in the whole league—and Chad hit eleven of them.*

He went out for football. When I played football, I was a running back, but Chad ended up on defense. I never dreamed that my son would one day be a starting tackle. By age fourteen he was already bigger than I am. He wears a size 12 shoe, he's flat-footed, and you wouldn't think he could run a lick, but he's the second-fastest runner on the football team. In high school they converted him to running back because he's big and fast.

Our daughter, Susan, is a recent high school graduate and

a super gymnast. She won a cheerleading scholarship to the University of California at Long Beach, where she is now studying business administration. It's nice to know that Susan is only a few miles from her brother Chris in Los Angeles. She loves art, fashion, and design, and she also seems to have unlimited energy. She is very athletic, an acrobatic tumbler, and like her brothers she has a lot of ambition and loves to compete.

Susan was a member of the all-star team, a group made up of the top cheerleaders from our area. They go through a series of regional competitions, and then the winners in each region compete at the national finals. Carolyn and I were very proud of Susan when her squad won the 1993 National Championship at the annual cheerleading competition in Dallas. And whether it's cheerleading, college, business administration, or any of her interests, Carolyn and I always want Susan to know that we love her and stand with her in the things she's doing. We try to give each of our kids that kind of support.

The Important Things

Support is important on the job as well, and just as I want my family to know that I care for them, I also hope all our people at the Charlotte Hornets know that I care for them, and I want to support them as well. When any of our players or staff have problems, I want them to know they can come to me and talk things over. Our head coach, Allan Bristow, is a professional, and he knows that if he ever has a gripe, he can come to me and talk it over. He'll say, "George, we need to talk." That's the way it should be. But once we reach a decision, we go with it. We may disagree at first, but once we reach a conclusion, we stand behind it together and keep a solid front.

I have said, "Allan, if you want something bad enough or if you believe in it strongly enough, then sell me on it. I am always open to your ideas. If it makes sense and you can show me that it will improve the team and that it's economically feasible, then I'm with you. But once we leave this room, whatever decision we've made, we've made it together. It's not George's decision, and it's not Allan's decision. It is *our* decision."

Allan agrees with that attitude. There have been times when we have had arguments, but that hasn't changed our relationship. I remember one occasion when we had a painful loss and several of us were in the coach's office together after the game. The assistant coaches were all there, along with our director of player personnel, and Allan lost it. He was very upset and started yelling at me, but I didn't say a word. I tried to be calm, and I said, "Allan, we'll talk about this tomorrow. We can't accomplish anything if we don't calm down and try to look at this thing from the right perspective." And that was the end of it.

The next day Allan came to me and said, "George, I'm sorry that I lost it yesterday. That was a tough loss, and I guess I just couldn't help myself."

I said, "That's all right, Allan. I know you were really down after the game, and I'm not going to get mad at you for blowing up like that. You might catch me at a bad time one of these days, and I might blow up at you, though I hope not. But I do understand and I do care, so let's put it behind us."

That's the kind of relationship we have. We have to support each other in this business, and it's important that we all keep in mind that we're in it together. During the 1993–94 season when the press was beating up on Allan day after day, I went out of my way to assure him that he had my support. Whenever I saw or heard that some reporter had been shooting at him or attacking the way he was handling the team, I went to him and said, "Allan, I heard what they said about you on TV today. Just remember, you don't work for those guys; you work for me, and I'm behind you all the way. Put it behind you and let's play basketball."

I would say, "Those newspaper and TV guys can't fire you, Allan, and George Shinn ain't gonna fire you. So you keep on doing what you can to get our players back in the win column, and the rest will take care of itself." I knew that the best way to silence our critics was to win basketball games, and I believed Allan could do that. So I said, "Your job is to keep the guys together and keep them focused." And I would add, "Keep them doing what they do best and we'll be all right."

I have never been upset with myself for having too much confidence in other people, and I have never been disappointed by being too loyal or too faithful to my friends. Whether it involves key employees, family members, close friends, or my business associates, I realize there will always be problems to deal with—that's the nature of life. But problems aren't the most important things; people are. Sooner or later, the problems will go away, but the relationships are for the long run.

16

Lessons of a Lifetime

PERHAPS the most interesting thing about my son Chris's growing-up experience was the way he found his niche in music. One Christmas, a good friend of mine named Arthur Smith came over to the house and spent some time with us. He told our kids all about what he does as a performer, and they thought that was great. In our part of the country, Arthur is well known as a country-western entertainer. Long before *Good Morning America,* he had one of the most popular morning shows in the state. They had it all: singers, dancers, comedy, old-fashioned gospel music, and wonderful family entertainment.

Over the years, we had developed a close friendship. Arthur was close to Johnny Cash and many of the country's top country-western stars, and of course, all of that made him very popular with our kids. That Christmas he brought Chris a very special present: a guitar. Chris fell in love with it immediately. He was about ten years old at the time. In no time, it seemed, Chris asked me if I would buy him an electric guitar, and I said, "Chris, Arthur gave you a nice guitar for Christmas. If you learn to play that one, then I'll buy you an electric guitar."

Well, one Sunday afternoon I was sitting in the den watching the football game when Chris came in with his guitar, which was bigger than he was at that time. He sat down on the floor and started picking quietly. All of a sudden I noticed that he was playing "Happy Trails to You," the old Roy Rogers theme song. I was shocked! Here was this ten-year-old kid, who had never had a lesson in his life, playing one of the songs I had grown up with. That really got my attention, so I said, "Chris, where did you learn to play that song?"

He said, "Oh, I heard it on the radio last night, Dad."

I said, "You heard it on the radio last night, and you picked it up and played it just like that?"

Needless to say, I bought him an electric guitar. I was absolutely impressed as I began to realize that Chris really had musical talent.

We have a large house with a large attic. When we built the house, we designed the attic to be big enough for three or four additional bedrooms. The idea was that when our youngest went off to college, we would take in maybe five or six foster kids, so our oversized attic was designed to be expandable as a sort of dormitory. We had plumbing going up there for bathrooms, and all the facilities were there to add rooms at some point. But for the moment it was just a large open space.

That seemed to be the perfect place for a music room, so we let Chris and his friends use the attic as their practice facility. People talk about having garage bands, and I suppose that's what Chris had, but his garage band was actually in the attic. They started a little rock band, and they practiced every day. Chris met a friend at church who played the keyboard; later they added a drummer and another guitar player. Eventually they were really making music. He started writing his own songs, and in no time, it seems, his band was getting invitations to play for high school dances and things like that.

My wife and I would go see them, like the other parents, and you know, we were really impressed. But what was most amazing was the way the other kids responded to him. They just loved him! You would have thought it was Elvis Presley the way they were screaming and hollering and carrying on.

It got to the point that Chris was so turned on to music that we wanted to make sure he didn't get in with the wrong crowd. We felt it was better for him to be upstairs at night in our own home than it would be to be out on the streets, so we encouraged Chris and the band to practice in the attic. They were there practically every night. The bad thing about it, though, was that Chris's music was becoming an obsession.

> *You would have thought it was Elvis Presley the way they were screaming and hollering and carrying on.*

His grades really started to suffer. It soon got to the point that his musical talents and his grades were going in opposite directions.

Carolyn and I did all we could to change the downward drift of his schoolwork. We tried rewards, threats, and everything we could think of to get him back into his studies, but it wasn't working. Charlotte Country Day School is an academically challenging school with university-caliber instruction in the upper grades, so Chris really had to work to keep up. When he was in the eleventh grade, it looked as if he was going to fail, so he asked if his mother and I would let him transfer to public school. He said that since public school was easier than private school, it wouldn't be quite as difficult to do his work there. We resisted for a while, then finally let him transfer. But that didn't help either.

As it turned out, changing schools was a mistake. Chris had already made up his mind that he wasn't going to do any more studying. The only thing he wanted in his life was music. He managed to make it to the twelfth grade, but his grades continued to slip. Then, a couple of months into his senior year, he got so depressed that Carolyn and I really began to worry about him.

One day he came to me and said, "Dad, I'm depressed, and I don't think I can handle it anymore." He had been thinking about this for a long time. He talked to me first, without his mom there, and asked me for permission to quit school. He knew how disappointed I would be, but he said that was what he wanted to do. I remembered how my mother had always told me that the one thing she wanted me to do more than anything else was to graduate from high school. I didn't know what else I could say now to my own son, although I hoped he would change his mind and stay in school.

I tried to draw on all my own resources and experiences to see what I could do to get him to hang on a little longer. It was only a matter of seven or eight months until he would graduate, if he could just buckle down for that long. By that time I knew that going to college was out of the question for him, but I wanted him to finish high school at least. Still, I agreed to think about it. We had a couple of meetings to talk it over, and I asked him to think about it for a while. I also promised that we would talk with his mom.

Hitting Home

When we all sat down together to talk about the situation, Chris said, "Dad, you know I've read your books, and I know what a lousy student you were in school. You're not really in much of a position to be telling me about the importance of making great grades, Dad!" That was one time when my stories about graduating last in my class didn't help me. Whenever I have given motivational talks to kids in our local schools, my story was always a great encourager. I always felt I was able to impress on young people the importance of a good education, but Chris was different. He wasn't buying it.

"Dad, I'm just like you," he said. "I have a dream. I know I'm young, and you and Mom think I'm just a kid, but it's clear in my mind. It's concrete. I know now what I am going to do with my life. I want to be in music more than anything in the world! Music is going to be my career, and nothing else will satisfy me.

"You can force me to stay in school," he said to us, "and you can make me take algebra and biology and French and all those subjects that won't help me. Sure, I'll go if you insist, but I'll be unhappy, because I won't be doing what I need to do to pursue my career in music. Dad, I want to write music. I want to continue to perform and produce my own stuff. It's in my blood. Music is my life—and it's going to be from now on."

I don't know if I had tears in my eyes while Chris was telling me all that, but I was torn inside. Half of me said, *He doesn't know what he's saying. He's so young and time seems so short to him now. There will be plenty of time for his career if he will just finish his education.* But the other half said, *He has a dream. And nothing is going to stop him from following that dream. I've been there, and I know how he feels.*

Chris said, "Mom, Dad, please see it my way. I'm committed to music, no matter what happens. I think I can be very good at it, but if I get married someday and have children and the only way I can feed my family is by singing and playing the guitar in a pub, then that's what I'm going to do. It means a lot to me." Little by little, he was bringing us around to his point of view. I realized that if I wanted him to get an education, I would have to do a little negotiating. I couldn't just say no, so I made him an offer.

I said, "All right, Chris, let's try and work through this thing together. First, I want you to know that I love you and I care about you very much. Your mother and I want you to be happy, and there's nothing that would please us more than for you to become the next Bruce Springsteen. Of course, I know the chances of that are very slim since there are thousands of young people out there right now with the same goal. But, in any case, if I let you quit school, you'll have to make me two promises.

"First," I said, "I want you to promise me that you will take and pass your GED as quickly as you can, through the community college system. Will you promise me that?"

"Yes, sir," he said.

"OK. Second," I said, "if we invest the money for you to stay somewhere close to the music industry so you can pursue your goal, you'll have to give me some realistic guarantees. For example, after a reasonable period of time, which we will determine at a later date, if it appears that you are not going to achieve the kind of success in the music business that you have in mind, then you'll come back home and go to college."

> "OK, Chris. You can quit school on those two conditions."

He agreed to that condition as well. So I said, "OK, Chris. You can quit school on those two conditions."

Chris quit school the next week, took his GED within six months, and actually received his high school diploma before the rest of his classmates. In fact, he passed his general equivalency exam and qualified for graduation on the first try.

Building a Career

We had continued to stay close to Arthur Smith, the guy who started all this with his guitar. We had also known his brother, Ralph Smith, who was a big hit on television. Ralph was a great guy, a comic, just full of wit and humor. Ralph had two sons we really admired, and one in particular was to become a big part of our lives.

Tim Smith had won a Morehead scholarship, which is one of the most prestigious academic awards anybody can receive in our part of the country. It's a full four-year scholarship to the University of North Carolina. But Tim, who is Ralph's son and Arthur's nephew, had turned down the scholarship because he couldn't study music—his chosen field—at the University of North Carolina. He went to the University of Miami to study music and graduated first in his class.

Tim Smith is also serious about his faith, and I especially remember a couple of things that happened when his father died. Ralph had told Tim that if he ever needed any help, he was to call on George Shinn. "George will give you a hand, Tim, so don't forget to call him if you're ever in a pinch." A few years after that, Tim was working on a music album. He came to me and said he needed $10,000 to be able to finish it, so I loaned him the money. We put together a timetable on how he would pay me back. He never missed a payment, and he paid it all back just as we agreed. That told me a lot about the kind of guy he is.

When my son Chris told me that, one way or another, he was going into the music business, I immediately thought about Tim. He was about thirty-five or so and a young man I really respected. I called him and said, "Tim, you know Chris wants to be a musician. Well, I'm not a good judge of that sort of thing, but I know you are. How about letting me pay you a monthly fee to work with Chris and his band, look over his music, and give me some advice on what I should do to try to help him.

"I don't want you to feel any personal obligation, Tim, just because we're friends of your family. If Chris doesn't have the talent to make it in the music business, please tell us. On the other hand, if he does have the talent to make a living at it, then give me some idea of what I can do to help him."

So we worked out an arrangement. Chris agreed to work with Tim for a while and see what they could make of his career. They hit it off immediately. They both loved music, and I felt better knowing that Tim, who is a very talented master musician, would be there to help guide Chris and give him advice.

Tim is one of the best bass guitarists I have ever heard. He not only knows how to play the guitar; he also understands music instinctively. He grew up with it in his family. He knows how to put on shows. He knows the radio and television end of it, the recording industry, all of it. He has been there.

After he had spent quite a bit of time with Chris, he came back and told me, "I know it's kind of hard for a parent to believe, particularly when they don't know too much about music themselves, that they have a very talented kid on their hands. But I think Chris has enormous talent, and I believe you should help him pursue a career in this field.

"It's true that the music industry is full of people with talent, but with your support, he might be able to make it out there. That might be the advantage he needs. He won't just be one of the faceless pack of musicians out there in the dark. He'll have a little bit of an edge because he's enormously talented, and besides that, he's your son."

I asked Tim to explain the "talented" part and why he felt that way. "Well, if you owned a record company, Mr. Shinn, what would you be looking for?"

"A new artist," I said.

"If you found a new artist who could play just about any type of stringed instrument—which Chris can—and could play the keyboards, the drums, and manage a band—which Chris can—do you think you would be interested?"

I said I thought I would be.

"Well," he continued, "what if he was somebody who could also tell the other artists how to play their parts even better and show them how to use their instruments better, and what if he was also nice looking, had a great voice, and on top of all that, wrote his own music. What would you say?"

"Tim, are you saying that Chris can do all of that?" I asked.

"That's right," he said. "And that's why I think Chris deserves a chance. What better candidate for getting a record contract could you have? It will cost you a little money, but what I would like to do is to take Chris out to Los Angeles and start trying to get him some introductions. We'll rent a first-class music studio, hire some of the best musicians we can get, and we'll cut a demo album. My brother, Roddy, will play lead guitar. In addition to Chris and me, we'll need a drummer, a keyboardist, and other backup people, but the best people in the business are all out there. Of course, we'll use some of the music that Chris has written, and then we will put that demo into the hands of people who can help us get things rolling."

"Your Son Is Talented"

That's just what they did. And while they were out there, Tim called a young man named Donnie Graves, who handles the business end of things and has worked for performers and groups like Sting, Michael Jackson's Victory Tour, the Fine Young Cannibals, Prince, and several others. Donnie came out to the studio while they were recording one afternoon, and afterwards he called me and asked if he could represent my son as his agent.

> *"You don't see too many eighteen-year-olds with that kind of talent."*

"Your son is talented," he said. "I was impressed not just with his performing and singing but with the way he directed the other musicians on the set. He would sit down at the drums and show the drummer, who was ten or fifteen years older than he was, the kind of sound he was looking for, and his technique really made the whole piece better. I thought that was pretty amazing, since that particular drummer is one of the best in the business. Then he did the same thing for the keyboardist and the guitarists. You don't see too many eighteen-year-olds with that kind of talent."

"All right, Donnie," I said, "but the next question is, if you want to represent him, how much money are you going to want?"

"I'm not going to charge you a penny, Mr. Shinn," he said.

207

"If I have any expenses traveling on his behalf, I would like you to reimburse me for that, but otherwise I won't charge you a cent. Once we get him under contract, I'll get a reasonable percentage of what Chris actually earns, but you won't have to pay me anything out of your pocket. My fee will come from what Chris makes, and then I'll be his agent and manage the business side of it for him."

Well, that's what sold me. I suspect a lot of people think I'm forking out some big bucks to get this big Hollywood agent to handle Chris, but that's not the case at all. And the best thing about his relationship with Chris is that Donnie and his wife, Donna, are nearby. Chris says they have been like a father and mother to him while he's away from home.

If I call out there and Chris isn't home, I just call Donnie or Donna, and they generally know where he is or where I can reach him. They love Chris like their own son. It has been a very positive relationship for all of us.

In spring 1995, Chris leased a great old house in Hollywood Hills that was originally built for Humphrey Bogart. The place is owned by Dean Torrence of the sixties rock group Jan and Dean. Dean has given him some pointers on the music business, and Chris says the place is the perfect environment for writing his songs. It must be working, because Chris recently signed a publishing contract with Chrysalis Music to develop and record some of his songs. Everybody's hoping this will be the start of something big.

Chris has a good shot at making it in music, but I know this time has also been a time of maturing, testing, and personal growth for him as well. In fact, something that happened during the Northridge earthquake in early 1994 probably helped me to have more confidence in him than ever before.

Early on the morning of January 17, 1994, a couple of friends in Charlotte called the house and asked me, "George, is Chris all right?"

"What are you talking about?" I said.

"Well, there was a major earthquake in Southern California early this morning, and we were worried about Chris. We just wanted to know if he's OK."

This was about eight o'clock, and needless to say that news woke us up immediately. I called Chris at his apartment, and he was still somewhat shaken by what had happened out there. I could hear his voice trembling as he said, "Dad, I have never been through anything like that before in my life. It was really scary."

Chris and the band had been out doing a gig until about three in the morning, he said. They were on the way home, and all of a sudden he couldn't feel the ground under the car. He has one of those big old four-wheel-drive vehicles with the huge wheels. He couldn't quite feel the actual shaking, but he knew something was strange about the way the car was handling. Then all of a sudden there were no lights. All the street lamps went out and it was pitch-black right in the middle of town.

"*I got down on my knees and, Dad, I just prayed.*"

"I didn't know what in the world had happened," he told me. "Out in the distance I could see explosions, fires, and flames shooting up into the sky. Things were just blowing up everywhere I looked." He said, "Dad, the first thing that went through my mind was, *Oh, no, we're being bombed!* I got out of the car and walked around to the front. I got down on my knees and, Dad, I just prayed."

I was deeply touched by his words. I thought, *You know, if this kid keeps this approach, he's going to be all right.* Obviously, we've got confidence in him. If he had gone to college, I might be spending more money on him than it's costing me to keep him living out there in California, and he's learning so much where he is right now. He's getting a tremendous education in the music business and in life, and he is doing what he really wants to do. Carolyn and I look at what he is doing as a great education for him.

I can't help but feel that it will work out for the best, one way or another, even if he doesn't make it to the big time.

Donnie is convinced he will make it, and he told me, "Even if he doesn't end up being an entertainer, he is definitely going to end up in music. He loves it so much, and he is such a natural talent." Time will tell. In the meantime, I want to give Chris and Susan and Chad all the support they deserve.

No Regrets

I feel that trust is so important in supporting my kids. Faithfulness and loyalty have always been major issues with me. If you trust someone, then you will give them a chance to try their wings and do what they feel they are called to do. We had to trust Chris when he was in junior high school and started letting his hair grow. That was a problem for us at first. He let it grow down to his shoulders, and then the next thing I knew he was wearing an earring. But trusting someone means accepting them as they are. When I was a kid, I did some things that were considered a little bit radical, and I survived.

I have found that the best way to build confidence and character in my kids is to let them know that I love them and trust them and that I expect the very best from them. So I try to give them a little bit of rope whenever I can. Every once in a while I have to tug it back in and give them some fatherly advice, but they are growing up and becoming young adults before my eyes, and I want them to develop their own sense of judgment.

I want my kids to know that, first and foremost, I love them, and I put them above the Charlotte Hornets. I put my family above anything I have, and it gives me pleasure to be able to help them. I learned an important lesson about that early on, when I was still working at one of the business schools a number of years ago. It was right around the time the Beatles were first starting out, and a young guy at the school started to let his hair grow out. He was sort of a radical kid—not a troublemaker, but more of a follower than a leader. He just thought it would be cool to let his hair grow out like the Beatles.

I remember his telling me that it was creating problems at home. His dad was a crew-cut type guy, and it was getting to the point where they were having battles every day. His father was screaming at him, threatening him, and calling him names. The kid also rode a motorcycle. This was back before the helmet laws came in, so he would ride to school and back on that motorcycle with his long hair blowing in the wind, and that seemed to make his family even more upset. If he had been my kid, I would have tried to talk him out of it too.

He was about twenty or so—maybe a little older, because he'd been out of school and had had several odd jobs before he came to the business college. He was starting to look a little ragged. After his hair grew out, he also started growing a beard, and it was even uglier than his hair. Things kept getting more and more terrible at home.

I always tried to stay close to my students, and this particular boy was having so many problems that I tried to meet with him from time to time just to see how he was coping. I would say, "Are you OK? Is there anything I can do to help?" But he never asked for anything.

One day he came home with a friend, and his father just lost it. He started cursing him, told him he was trash, and said, "You are not my son. You don't belong in this house. Get out!" At that point he physically pushed him out of the house and told him never to come back.

His father told him he could pick up his clothes the next day, but after that he was never to come back to that house again. "You don't belong to me," his father told him. "You're trash, and I'm through with you."

It wasn't long after that, no more than a week or two, that this young fellow was out on his motorcycle when it started to rain. The pavement was slick, and just as he was going across a railroad track, he lost control of the bike, fell off, and slammed his head against one of the cross ties. He was killed instantly. I remember seeing his father at the funeral. He was a big man with a short crew cut. He was a big tough fellow, and he just stood near the back of the room for a while. As I was walking up to view the body, his father came up at the same time.

I couldn't believe what happened next. The man reached down and put his hand into the casket. He ran his fingers through his son's long hair and reached down and ran his hand over his beard—and he just started bawling. Tears were streaming down his face as he looked at his son's lifeless body. And he said, "Son, I love you."

The emotion in that chapel was overwhelming. It was almost more than I could take. I wanted to embrace this man and try to say something to comfort him, but I couldn't come up with the words. Everyone there that day knew what had been going on in that family. It was so clear now that the father truly loved his son. He wanted the boy to know how much he cared and how sorry he felt for the things he had said. But he had waited too long to tell him. And he lost him.

> I wanted to embrace this man and try to say something to comfort him, but I couldn't come up with the words.

Pulling Together

It was too late for that father to admit that he had made a mistake. It was too late to ask his son to come back home. He wasn't to blame for killing the boy, but you couldn't convince him of that fact. The accident was a crushing blow. Perhaps he never recovered; I don't know. That was a tragedy I witnessed with my own eyes.

There is a world of difference between that situation and my relationship with my son Chris, but sometimes when I think I would prefer for him to come home and live a more normal life, I remember that scene. I don't want to tell my son that he has to do what I want him to do or be what I expect him to be. Some of his views are different from mine, but he's an adult now and he has a right to discover his own way. I want him to live his life the best way he knows how. I also want to help him, and I want to be a part of his life as a father and a friend. And above all, I want all three of my children to know that I love them very much.

Chris never fails to tell me and his mother that he loves us whenever he calls home. Not many kids will do that, particularly when they're twenty years old and trying to make their own way in the world, but that's the type of relationship we have. I think that is also the type of relationship everybody needs to have with their family.

When I think about all the lessons I've learned over a lifetime, I don't think there are any more important than these: Trust people to do their best. Encourage them with your support. And let them know you appreciate them for doing the right thing.

There may well be times when you are disappointed in other people, and you may not win all the time. But when you learn to express your trust and confidence in people and when you show them your support by being faithful, things have a way of working out for the best. And it sure makes life more enjoyable.

17

The Look of a Winner

DURING the time I was pursuing the Hornets franchise, one of the first things I did was to meet with the architects who had designed the Charlotte Coliseum and were supervising construction of our new facility. They wanted to show me the color charts and all the various plans for what they were going to do, and I was eager to see what the arena would look like.

I had already been informed by Norm Sonju, the general manager at Dallas, that we should plan to tie together the color scheme of the seats and the uniforms if we wanted to have a good-looking team. When I went over to see all those plans, I was just flabbergasted. What I saw impressed me very much.

The designers had decided that the basic colors would be teal, Carolina blue, and pink. I had never seen that combination of colors used together, but I thought that teal and pink was a beautiful combination and I loved it. A few years ago I might have thought they were sissy colors and not the kind of thing you would want for a professional basketball team, but I liked what I saw and I was sold on it.

That inspired me. I thought, *You know, we are going to have a new coliseum with beautiful colors, beautiful appointments, and a spectacular facility for our team, and we could end up being on nationwide television several nights a week.*

I began wondering if there might not be some famous designer who could help us design our new uniforms.

> I called Alexander Julian as soon as I got back to my office and told him I was delighted he wanted to work with us.

Then I remembered that Max Muhleman, the guy who had produced the sensational video and promotional materials that helped us win the franchise, had told me once that fashion designer Alexander Julian is from our state, and he would be great. "That's right," I said, "I had forgotten all about that. He's just the guy we need. I mean, half the sweaters in my closet are Alexander Julian designs!"

I wasn't sure how to reach Alex in New York, so Max called a friend at Nations Bank, which was the bank we were dealing with at that time, to see if they had any contacts with Alex or his family. "Well, sure," they said, "we do the banking for his father, who still owns the clothing store in Chapel Hill where Alexander Julian got his start."

"That's wonderful," Max said. "Do you mind calling Mr. Julian to find out if his son would be interested in designing our new Hornets uniforms?"

They agreed to make the contact for us, and within a

matter of only a day or two we got a call back from the folks at the bank. They said that Mr. Julian had called his son in New York, and Alexander was excited about the chance to work with us. "Alexander would love to do it," they said, and they gave me his direct number in New York.

Into the Briar Patch

I called Alexander Julian as soon as I got back to my office and told him I was delighted he wanted to work with us. I had been wearing his shirts and sweaters for years. I told him, "Alex, I would love for you to design our uniforms and help with the colors, but I have one special request. I would like for you to make sure that the primary color is teal."

He just started laughing. I wasn't quite sure why, but then he said, "Do you know how Brer Rabbit felt when they threw him in the briar patch, George?"

"He was pretty excited about it, as I remember," I said.

"Well, that's how I feel," he said. "Most people say that teal is *my* color. That's perfect, and I think it's a great choice for your team. I assure you, I'll be happy to work around that color." So that's how it started, and eventually we made it even more distinctive. Alex felt that the shade of teal selected by the coliseum designers didn't have quite enough blue in it. He changed it slightly, and today we call that particular shade "Hornets teal."

I told him, "If you want to use the pink, that's fine too. The pink will tie in with the coliseum colors, and quite frankly, you won't offend me!" Then I said, "Another thing I would like to do is to change the uniforms a little bit. I would like see if we can make the top more like a T-shirt with sleeves as opposed to the tank tops most of the other teams are wearing. Do you think you could do something with that idea?"

When he started to design the uniforms, Alex had some people go out and shoot baskets with different types of uniforms to see which styles and shapes worked best on the court. If the T-shirts restricted movement or anything like that, then he would have to make some modifications, but before long they concluded the new design would work just fine.

However, as it turned out, the look of the shirts wasn't the main concern. They had to be certain that the players would be comfortable in them, and they discussed whether the fact that the Hornets would be the only team in the league wearing a T-shirt design might not affect the players mentally. After talking with several players, they decided that the T-shirt would be too much of a switch, so we decided to stay with the traditional tank jersey.

Then they wanted to know if the idea of wearing pink might affect the players in any way. Alex said, "In the beginning, when your team will be losing a lot of games, you sure don't want anybody calling them sissies because they're wearing pink. If it's OK with you, George, I think I would rather go with teal and purple. That combination really works well together, particularly with vertical stripes." He showed me a sample of the colors together, and, bingo, that's how the uniforms our players use today came about.

In the coliseum, the pink is mostly in the signs. When you're walking around the concourse and the snack bar and places like that, you will see pink in the signs and some of the striping and a few other things like that. We are very happy with the color combination, and most people seem to think it has turned out to be just the right combination for the Hornets.

Response from our fans and the media has all been positive. Alexander Julian held a press conference in New York to introduce the uniforms, and all the fashion editors came out to see what he had done. It was really something to behold. There was a picture of Alex in the *San Francisco Chronicle*—a huge color picture showing the Hornets from little ol' Charlotte all decked out in these handsome new uniforms. Basketball uniforms by international design sensation Alexander Julian! That was just one more indication of the uniqueness of this team.

One Mean Bug!

We got incredible press coverage from that event, and the news was very positive for the team. After that success, I asked Alex to help us design our team logo. He called a friend, a graphic designer, to come over and meet with us.

He asked me, "What kind of logo do you want? What are the main elements you are interested in? Do you want a basketball in it? Do you want it to be cartoonish? Do you want it to be action or static?" He had a ton of questions like that.

"Well," I said, "I just want it to be *one mean bug.*"

Alex still teases me about that "one mean bug." But we began to brainstorm on that idea. We thought of all the ways you could illustrate a bee in a single compact design.

"You know," I said, "if we could have a bee that's really upset and flying through the hoop with a basketball in his hand, that might work. I mean, that's a *mean bug.* Do you see what I mean?"

The designer laughed. "Yeah, I get your drift." He came back with a drawing in the shape of an H that combined the main elements of the design I had described. At the top of the H was a basketball hoop, and above it was a bee with a stinger slamming down through the basket, tearing it all to pieces.

That was a good first effort, but it didn't quite have the feeling I wanted. Maybe my suggestion of "one mean bug" made him come off a little too angry or not quite as appealing as I had hoped it might be. I called my close friend and partner Rick Hendrick, who was just getting into the racing-car business at that time, to see if he had any ideas. Of course, Rick's NASCAR team is one of the best in racing today, and his driver, Jeff Gordon, and his crew are tops. The race team was designing and selling their own T-shirts for race drivers, and they had an in-house artist who did most of their work. I asked Rick if he thought his guy might be able to help us. He gave me his name and telephone number, and we set up a meeting.

I tried to describe what I had in mind, but once again I wasn't happy with the first effort. He did several sketches of yellow jackets, but that wasn't the look I wanted. We talked some more, and this time he came back with just what I was hoping for. The minute I saw it, I knew he had come up with the perfect design for our Hornet. Today, that figure is known as "Hugo the Hornet." The only problem with the first drawing was that the bug was still yellow and brown, like a yellow jacket.

I said, "I like this figure a lot, but this bug has got to be teal and purple. We can't have a yellow jacket. This is a *teal hornet!*"

He said, "OK, I've got you now." He had his little box of colored pencils in his case, so he took out another drawing and colored it in, putting teal and purple in the stripes and darkening in the eyes, and when he finished, I said, "That's it! You've done it. This is just what I wanted. Now put a basketball in his hand, and you've got the perfect Hornet!"

"Who is the best mascot builder in the world?" I asked.

I called Alex and sent him a copy of the new drawing. I said I was going to use the first logo his friend had done as a marketing symbol, and the second one, the Hugo image, would be our official mascot. But when the NBA saw it, they told me I couldn't have two symbols. "You've got to let us know which one is going to be your official logo," they said. So I sent both pictures around to all our employees, players, and staff, and asked which one they liked best.

They looked at the drawing of the hornet with the basketball, and then they looked at the one of the old stinger going through the hoop, and their decision was unanimous. There was no question that they all liked the Hugo drawing the best. That's the way I felt too, so we informed the NBA of our choice.

Once again I called Alex and told him I was looking for some help in developing our team mascot. We had done everything in the most professional way we could in putting together our colors and symbols and design elements, and now I wanted to do the same thing with our mascot design. "Who is the best mascot builder in the world?" I asked. "And if we can find out who that is, do you think we can get him to make us a hornet?" Our hornet wasn't actually named Hugo at that time—we wouldn't come up with the name until some time later—but that was the image we had in mind. Alex asked me to let him think about it for a few days, and he said he would call me back with the name of the best mascot designer.

Sure enough, about a week later I got a call back and Alex said, "George, have you ever heard of Jim Henson?"

I said, "Are you kidding? Of course I have. He's the creator of the Muppets and one of the most outstanding character designers in the country!"

He said, "What would you think if we could get him to do your mascot for you?"

"He is the best," I said. "I would really love that, Alex."

He said, "You're right, he is the best. But do you want to pay the kind of money he is going to charge you to design your mascot? Are you sure you want to pay someone as famous as Jim Henson to do it?"

"Call and ask him," I said. "Find out how much he'll charge, and that will tell me if I want Henson to do it."

When Alex called me back, he said that Henson was willing to do it for us. His price was very high, but that wasn't the main problem. The problem was that Henson's firm wanted to own all trademarks for the characters they produced. If he designed our mascot, we wouldn't own the Hornets trademark anymore. I couldn't agree to that.

"No way," I said. "That character belongs to the Charlotte Hornets, not the Muppets or Jim Henson. And building a foam rubber character from our design isn't a good enough reason for us to give away the rights to our mascot."

Alex made another call to Henson, and when he called back this time, he said that Henson would not do it under

221

those conditions. However, he said, Henson's daughter could make the mascot for us if we were interested. His daughter, Cheryl, had grown up with the Muppets, and she was involved in making several of their most famous characters.

I said, "That would be great, Alex. It will still have the Henson touch, and that will make it special enough, don't you agree?"

"You're right, George," Alex said. "No matter which Henson does it, you will be getting the best in the world." We met with Cheryl, and she knew exactly what we wanted. I told her I wanted the character to look just like the picture—same colors and everything—and that's what she did.

In Living Color

Cheryl Henson not only designed and built the Hugo costume to our design, but she built it to fit a particular person she wanted us to hire as the team mascot. The young man she recommended came down and tried out for us, and everybody agreed he did an incredible job.

Once the season actually began, he moved down to Charlotte and got an apartment nearby. He spent hours working out and developing his routine. He did a terrific job for us until he started missing various special events. He always made it to the games, but sometimes he wouldn't show up for some of the other functions. People would pay for him to attend grand openings, school parties, and various civic events. He was a great dancer, so he became enormously popular with the fans, but when he missed some of those things, we had to warn him that his job was on the line. The situation didn't improve after a reasonable period of time, so we let him go and hired a new Hugo to take over the job.

As it turned out, the new guy was even more athletic than our first Hugo. He was more of a gymnastic performer. He plays not only Hugo but another character we call Super Hugo, which is Hugo in a skintight outfit like Superman's. He uses the springboard and does slam dunks. He flies up in the air, does flips, and performs some of the most incredible things you could imagine with a basketball. The fans just love him, and he is one incredible athlete.

There is a national mascot competition each year at the All-Star Game, and our Hugo has won it ever since the first year we entered the contest. After he won it three years in a row, they refused to invite him back, because they wanted to give some of the other mascots a chance, but we think the NBA has been terribly unfair. He just happens to be the best in his field, and he shouldn't be penalized for that. That's what the NBA is all about.

Everyone should be allowed to do what they do best, and nobody should put barriers or roadblocks in front of people who are trying to do a good job. As owner, I try to carry that attitude to the games with me. If I go to the dressing room before or during a game, I try not to interfere with the coaches but just to be there to shake hands with the guys and tell them, "Have a good game tonight. Play hard," and to give them a little encouragement.

> **Everyone should be allowed to do what they do best.**

After the game, if they win, I like to go down and congratulate them and tell them how proud I am of the way they played. But if they lose, I know some of the guys are going to be down, so I usually just drop by and tell them, "Good game. Thanks for giving your best effort." Sometimes I'll say, "You played your heart out—don't let it get you down. We can't win 'em all, but we'll be back for the next one." I don't complain, I don't yell, and I try never to give the coaches a hard time. They put enough pressure on themselves without my adding to it, and I feel that my job is to give them support and encouragement.

As a motivational speaker and an entrepreneur, I am always preaching hope. That's my main theme, and I say that if you have hope, you will have opportunity. If you lose hope, then you've lost everything, because without that, you can't succeed. It all begins with hope. No matter how far down you may get, there's always hope. It's an old saying, but it's true: When you hit bottom, the only way to go is up.

A lot of people around the country seem to like the Hornets, and they see us as a team of the future. With the combination of Larry Johnson as "Grandmama"—a comic role he plays sometimes for the fans, dressed up in a granny gown and a wig—and with Muggsy Bogues as the little man with the giant-sized heart, I think we offer a lot of quality entertainment and excitement on the court.

Larry Johnson and Glen Rice can play with the best of them. Scott Burrell is a top defensive player and a big part of the team, and along with each of our starters and backups, there is a lot of appeal to our game. The Hornets are a big draw for basketball fans all over the country.

When you're a young team with a lot of money and a lot of people pulling for you, people notice. It makes me happy that so many people have taken a liking to the Hornets. They like our team logo, our team colors, and a lot of things like that. You might be surprised how many sports fans around the country are wearing our team jerseys and ball caps.

When they go to pick out a shirt or hat, a lot of times they will pick our team because they like the colors and the design. Thanks to our success, the purple-and-teal has the look of a winner, and when they see that Alexander Julian look, a lot of people will say, "Hey, that's the one I want. Those are great colors." And right there another Charlotte fan is born.

18

Believing Is the Bottom Line

BEING a popular and successful team gives us a lot of opportunities to have an outreach to the community. For several
years now I have supported the men's homeless shelter in
Charlotte, and I have been a major donor to charities that
touch the disadvantaged or disabled members of our community. I served as chairman of the capital campaign drive
for the Boy Scouts of America in Mecklenburg County. I have
been involved with the YMCA, and of course, I am very active
in the development campaign for Barber-Scotia College.

For the men's shelter each Christmas, I buy shoes for all
the residents. We preorder them, and some of the players

and staff go down with me to size the shoes for each of the men in the shelter. We give them new socks and shoes on Christmas Day—as we have been doing every Christmas for the past five years—and many people seem to feel that this is a good way for us to express our concern for the less fortunate.

We also put together big baskets of food, with turkeys and all kinds of good things, and give them to needy families. The Social Services Department tells us which are the most needy homes, and we drive out there on Christmas Day and distribute all these things. Several of our players go out, some of the local police officers go along with us, and we take the food right up to the door. It's a wonderful experience for all of us. Most of these families have kids, and they just can't believe that the star players from the Hornets would care about them like that. But they do.

> "They're going to look at what you've accomplished—not just how good a player you are, but how good a person you are."

It's true, our players are very successful and very good at what they do for a living. They are among the luckiest men in America, and I try to help them remember just how privileged they are. They are so fortunate to be athletes in this league, to be one of just 350 other men who can play in the NBA and make the kind of money they make. That's why we try to give back to the community. When you have been blessed as we have been blessed, the only reasonable response is to try to be a blessing to others. Most of our players agree with that philosophy, and they try to reach out to other people who need a hand.

Whenever I'm trying to get points like that across to them on how important it is to give back, I say, "If you reach out to get involved with good causes and charities, people will see that, and they will respect you for your generosity. I know a lot of you guys think you're immortal and you're going to play this game forever, but that's not going to happen. You can't play basketball forever, and you might be out of the game by the time you're thirty-five years old while you're still a very young man.

"You may have a college degree," I tell them, "but you don't have any experience in the real world. Some of these big companies might want to hire you in public relations or some other field, but they're going to look at what you've accomplished—not just how good a player you are, but how good a *person* you are. So there's no better time than now to start doing those things to help other people, which may also benefit you someday in the future."

But you know, lessons like that apply to everyone, not just professional athletes. If you're rude and arrogant and you take advantage of people, who's going to want to help you? Nobody will want to lift you up if you've been shoving people down your whole life. The people who get a helping hand are the ones who help others and who reach out to do a good deed, even when nobody else is watching. In fact, I would say *especially* when nobody else is watching, because there is one Somebody who is always watching.

Words of Wisdom
There are more than enough things to disappoint us and wound us as we go through life, but most of the time, the smart thing to do is to just overlook those things and go on with a sense of confidence and self-determination. I sometimes use the expression, "You can get bitter or you can get better," and as far as I'm concerned, I don't have time for bitterness.

Life is too short to waste on the small stuff. I have had one stroke, and I have faced the possibility of having it all end right in the middle of the game. Today, I want to do whatever I can to stay above the squabbles and the feuds, and I would like to help as many people as I can to reach their dreams and discover the thrill of success.

I said it earlier, that you always have to look for the upside of a down situation. I know that's not always easy. Sometimes life can be very painful. All over this country there are people struggling under very difficult circumstances, and I know many of them can't imagine being optimistic about anything. But good fortune has as much to do with attitude as it does with money or opportunity or lucky breaks. If you have a positive attitude and if you just refuse to let the bad breaks hold you down, then nothing can stop you.

During the darkest days of World War II, when it looked like England was going to be overrun by the Nazis and there was just no way their weak and outnumbered forces could resist the enemy, Winston Churchill was asked to speak at the boys' school he had attended as a child. He drove all the way up from London and arrived just in time to speak—and he gave the strangest speech anyone in that room had ever heard.

He said, "Never give in." That's all. He didn't just say it once. He looked out across that room full of boys and men, some of whom would likely go off to war very soon—many of whom might be dead in a matter of weeks—and he said, "Never give in." And to emphasize the point he repeated it again, "Never, never, never, never—in nothing, great or small, large or petty—never give in except to convictions of honor and good sense." It wasn't the speech anyone expected; in fact, many wondered if something had gone wrong with the prime minister. He said a few more words and sat down.

There was a moment of tense silence in the room, but as the impact of those simple words sank in, they all knew what that great man was saying. The war was terrible, and it would get even worse. Many would die; they might even lose the war. But win or lose, the only proper attitude for an Englishman was defiance in the face of evil. Those words, which have now gone down in history and have been repeated tens of thousands of times over the last fifty years, still ring as powerfully today as they did then. No matter how tough it may be, no matter how terrible you may feel, no matter how desperate the odds against you may be, *never give in.*

During the 1994–95 season, the Charlotte Hornets have had to remind themselves to hold on through the tough times and to just keep doing the best they can against long odds. A couple of our local reporters wrote stories on several occasions saying that we would never make the play-offs, but that didn't stop us.

We believed we could do it, and we didn't intend to be stopped by the negative words of people who by all rights should be our biggest supporters. And even when the media gets down on us, the fans know what we can do. If we can keep all our guys healthy, we're going to be hard to beat, year after year after year. We have no intention of ever giving in.

Larry Johnson, Alonzo Mourning, and several of our star players were injured in the 1993–94 season and were out of action for several weeks. But by the end of the season they were back and coming on strong. If you take that season and divide it into thirds, you can see just how powerful we were as a team. At the beginning of the season when we had all our players, we played tremendous basketball. Many people thought we would win the division. In the middle of the season, however, our two big horses were out with injuries and we even lost some of our key backups—we had a rash of injuries for a while there. But in the final third of the season, they all came back and we began to hit our stride.

If you look at our win-loss record during the times that our players were healthy, we had the fourth-best team in the entire NBA. Nobody can win when their star players are out, but we know that if we can keep a healthy team all season, then buckle up your seat belts, fans. You're going to be in for one exciting ride!

229

Giving It Up

Sometimes people ask me, "George, why do you keep on doing this? You're under a lot of stress, you've already had one stroke, and the media give you no end of problems.

Why do you do it?" One of my closest friends said, "You know, George, you could sell this team for a lot of money. You paid $30 million for it, but some of the expansion teams are going for $150 million these days, and you could probably get more than that for the Hornets. So why don't you just sell it, buy yourself a place in the islands, and spend the rest of your life in peace and happiness?" For that kind of money I suppose I could buy a whole island, but I told him—as I have told everyone—that giving it up is not in my plans.

I said, "You know, the surprises and the excitement involved with running a team like this are part of the fuel that keeps me going. If I sold the team, I would have to find something else to do." I don't believe in retiring. I have seen too many statistics that show that when people retire from the jobs they love, they die. That's not what I have in mind.

When I speak to groups of older people, I always say, "It's all right to retire from your job, but don't retire from life. Keep busy, keep going, keep doing something! Whether it's volunteer work or running a business of your own, keep busy." People can be involved in church work, civic organizations, or just about anything else. Regardless of their age, they can help others while doing themselves a favor. "Help others and you help yourself," I tell them, "and you will live longer too. Statistics prove that."

When the Hornets made the play-offs at the end of the 1992–93 season, we were only in our fifth year—which is almost unheard of. When I first predicted that we would make it our fifth year, everybody said I was crazy. Then all of a sudden I became this great philosopher and prophet. But, you know, it was easy for me to do. I made that prediction by simple deduction when we first got the franchise. I asked myself, *Who was the last team to get a franchise?* It was Dallas. So I picked up the phone and called their general manager, Norm Sonju. Other than Mayor Harvey Gantt, you'll recall that Norm was the person who helped me more than anybody else in getting the team.

Norm had given me good advice about when to speak up and when to keep my mouth shut, and he told me lots of things that helped me get a feel for life in the NBA. I invited him to come down as a speaker at one of our meetings, and we became real good friends. I still think the world of him. At that time, Dallas had the model franchise. Some unfortunate things have happened since then, and I think they made some bad decisions along the way, but that happens. If they hang in there, they'll recover.

I remember talking to Norm when we first came into the league and asking him, "Norm, how long did it take you guys to make it to the play-offs?"

"Five years," he said.

So I thought, *Why shouldn't I say that we could do the same thing? I mean, if they did it in five, we can do it in five. We're every bit as good a team as they are.* So when people asked me, I said that we would make the NBA play-offs in five years. The press went wild. They said, "Either this guy is crazy, or he's on something. He believes the Hornets can be in the playoffs in their fifth season!" But then we did it, and they began to change their tune.

> When people asked me, I said that we would make the NBA play-offs in five years.

Not only did we make the play-offs, but we beat the mighty Boston Celtics in the first round. Then we played New York and lost to them four games to one—but the excitement of being in the play-offs in only our fifth season was so high that the city of Charlotte acted as if we had won the world championship. They threw a big parade for the team, and on the front page of the *Charlotte Observer* the next day was a picture of me and Allan Bristow riding through uptown Charlotte in an open convertible. That was a great moment.

So even our harshest critics finally had to say that there is something going on in Charlotte, and this may very well be a team of destiny. It meant a lot for all of us—players, coaches, staff, management, and fans alike—and it did more to charge our batteries than anything else.

A Team of Destiny

I have talked about this team's being a team of destiny for a long time. I have told the journalists and reporters, "I don't care what you guys think, or what you write about us, or what you say about this team. I believe this is a team of destiny, and I have believed it since long before I got the franchise. I believed it then and I believe it now. I don't know why, but when I look at all the facts and how we got to this point, I just can't help the gut reaction and the feeling I get. I believe this team is going to be one of the top teams in the NBA very soon, mark my words."

We are heading in that direction right now, and I'm a firm believer that you're going to see some exciting things happening in Charlotte in the months ahead. The reporters all said, "Well, you just got lucky last year, Shinn. You got the number one pick and the number two pick in the lottery, and that was just luck."

"Well, call it luck if you like," I said, "but let me tell you something about luck. Luck happens when people are working hard and doing the right stuff. I believe those little balls that were bouncing around in there were controlled by something bigger than luck, and that something—or Someone—is bigger than you or I. That's what controls those balls."

Whether you believe it or not, and no matter how hokey it may sound, I believe it. You can call it luck, but I say it was a Higher Power that controlled where those balls would land. When you have good people and when you work together like a family, that creates a bond and a certain chemistry that can't help but have a good effect. There's a special power in that sort of relationship.

To be a team of destiny, I think we have to have a special vision and a special commitment to the people who support us. A team of destiny is one that has divine guidance, and I think we do. We are the only team that shows reverence the way we do; we're the only team that shows respect for our national anthem and our flag. I certainly don't mean to suggest that other teams are disrespectful—that is not the case at all. But what I mean is that we actively and deliberately salute the flag and we actively and deliberately include prayer at the start of each game and make faith an important part of the life of our team.

Along with these things, we have a great base of support with our local fans, who continue to buy season tickets year after year. The people of North and South Carolina continue to support this team, and as a result of all that, a lot of the other players in the league would love to come here and play for this club.

Keeping Your Focus

Going to the play-offs and being a top contender every season is a confidence builder. That's the way we like to operate. You've got to dream a little bit, and then you've got to plan to get there. Whether you're a player or a fan or a youngster in school, if you want to reach your goals, you've got to write them down and work at it every single day. Goals aren't achieved by accident, and most of the time luck is highly overrated. Write out your goals and spell out your dreams. You can't make a thousand-mile journey without a road map, and you will never achieve your goals unless you know where you're headed.

> You've got to dream a little bit, and then you've got to plan to get there.

You need to remind yourself each day, "I've got to do *this* today so I can do *that* tomorrow. And if I do that and keep taking one step at a time, it's going to bring me closer to my goal." This principle holds true no matter what you do for a living or what you're shooting for. Whether you're in sales or in management, or whether you're a schoolteacher or a kid in a band, if your goal is to make money, then decide what it will take for you to make the amount of money you hope to earn. "All I've got to do to earn this much money," you might say, "is to sell this amount of widgets. In the first year, I've got to sell this many, and the second year, this many more." Don't wait until the last month to try to sell them. You can't make up for lost time, so make a plan and keep at it, moving forward the best way you can.

I always encourage people to start now with that dream they've always wanted to pursue. Unfortunately, most people don't do that. I'm convinced that I am where I am today because I planned to be here. I didn't make my plan last week. I planned to be where I am now years ago. I had a dream, and I put some muscle behind that dream, and I accomplished my dream with the help of a lot of good people.

In the 1993–94 season, the Charlotte Hornets went through the frustration of losing two superstars to injuries, and that hurt us big time. One of our local reporters says he got sick of hearing me say it, but overcoming long odds motivates me and makes me want to work just that much harder. It doesn't bother me in the least to make him sick, so I'll probably keep on saying it: When we're down and every-body else is saying we're out of it, I want to play just that much harder and prove that we can do the job.

One of these days, sooner than a lot of people think, we are going to make it to the top. We will not only make it to the play-offs, but we're going all the way. And after that we'll keep on going, because we believe we can do it. I have done a lot of things in business, and all things considered, I've enjoyed the journey from Kannapolis to the NBA. I can't imagine any business I'd rather be in. We have to face new challenges every day. We are constantly fighting brush fires with certain people or with the media or with the other teams in the league, but that only increases the excitement and the ad-venture of what we're doing.

When I started this book, I described the early days of my

234

youth, and I said that one day I discovered that commitment, determination, hard work, and self-discipline could change the quality of my life and help me accomplish all the things I really wanted to do. I guess that is really the point of my story. I made up my mind that I was going to be the best I could be. Even though I have stumbled more times than I can count, I wouldn't change a thing. I have learned a lot about myself, and I've learned even more about other people and the way we can multiply our achievements when we work together for the common good.

The important thing for me today is to keep the focus, to try to build on the strong foundations I've already established, and to keep moving in a positive direction from here on out. The message I give is simple, but I think it is vital. If you have your priorities in order and you understand your relationship first to God, then to your family, and then to all the other people who are so important for a full and happy life, you will have a proper balance in your life. From there on, it is just a matter of concentration.

Learn from your experiences. Put the bad stuff behind you, and keep on working to achieve your goals. Once you have your priorities straight, nothing can stop you. But you've got to believe. This is the most important lesson of all. Whatever you do, don't lose your faith. You *gotta* believe!